THE SEVEN RAYS

A THEOSOPHICAL HANDBOOK

BY

ERNEST WOOD

Third Edition

THEOSOPHICAL PUBLISHING HOUSE

ADYAR, MADRAS, INDIA

1928

SOLD BY
THE KROTONA BOOK SHOP
OJAI, CALIFORNIA

COPYRIGHT

First   printed : 1925
Second Edition : 1926
Third   Edition : 1928

CONTENTS

PART I

THE SOURCE OF THE RAYS

PART II

THE SEVEN RAYS

PART III

THE GREAT USE AND DANGER OF KNOWLEDGE OF THE RAYS

THE SOURCE OF THE RAYS

There are seven Forces in Man and in all Nature. The real substance of the Concealed [Sun] is a nucleus of Mother-Substance. It is the Heart and Matrix of all the living and existing Forces in our Solar Universe. It is the Kernel from which proceed to spread on their cyclic journeys all the Powers that set in action the Atoms, in their functional duties, and the Focus within which they again meet in their Seventh Essence every eleventh year. He who tells thee he has seen the Sun, laugh at him, as if he had said that the Sun moves really onward in his diurnal path. . . .

It is on account of this septenary nature that the Sun is spoken of by the ancients as one who is driven by seven horses equal to the metres of the Vedas; or, again, that, though he is identified with the seven Gana [Classes of Being] in his orb, he is distinct from them, as he is, indeed; as also that he has Seven Rays, as indeed he has. . . .

The Seven Beings in the Sun are the Seven Holy Ones, self-born from the inherent power in the Matrix of Mother-Substance. It is they who send the seven principal Forces, called Rays, which, at the beginning of Pralaya, will centre into seven new Suns for the next Manvantara. The energy from which they spring into conscious existence in every Sun is what some people call Vishnu, which is the Breath of the Absoluteness.

Occult Aphorisms, quoted in THE SECRET DOCTRINE

CHAPTER I

THE PILLAR OF LIGHT

I SEE no means to avoid, in the writing of this book, and the putting forth of what I hope are clear ideas about the Rays, certain matters of a rather abstract character, and foremost among them a statement about the universality of God or Brahman, whom some regard as living far away on a high plane somewhere beyond our vision. The fact is that the Sachchidânanda Brahman [1] is here and now, before us and with us every day. Analyse the entire world of your experience, and you will find that it is composed of three parts: there is first a great mass of objects of all kinds, which are material on every plane, however high; secondly, there are vast numbers of living beings, with consciousness evolved in various degrees; and thirdly, there is yourself. The first of these three is the world of sat, existence; the second is that of chit, consciousness; and the third is ânanda, happiness, the true self.

This will be better understood if we recall the story of the great pillar of light. The great being Nârâyana, Vishnu, the soul and life of the Universe, thousand-eyed and omniscient, was reclining upon his couch, the body of the great serpent Sesha or Ananta, endless time, which lay coiled up on the waters of space, for it was the night of being. Then

[1] The term Brahman, neuter, applies to the entire trinity of Shiva, Vishnu and Brahmâ, but Brahmâ, masculine, is the third member of that trinity.

Brahmâ, the great creator of the world of being, called sat, came to him and touched him with his hand, and said: "Who art thou?" And an argument arose between those two as to who was the greater, and while this was going on, and as it threatened to become furious, there appeared before them a great pillar of fire and light, incomparable and indescribable, which astonished the disputants so much that they forgot their quarrel and agreed to search for the end of so wonderful a thing. Vishnu plunged downwards for a thousand years, but he could not find its base, and Brahmâ flew upwards for a thousand years, but he could not find its top, and both returned baffled. Then Shiva, whose nature is ânanda, stood before them and explained that they two were one in him their overlord, the pillar of light, who was three in one, and that in the coming age Brahmâ would be born from Vishnu, and Vishnu should cherish him, until at the end of it they both should see their overlord again.

People sometimes think that by going upwards they may find God, but the truth is that even were they to go downwards below their present state and search for a thousand years they could not find the end of Him. This does not mean that He is here but invisible and unknown to us. He is here visible and known; for the world that we see with our eyes is His sat, and the consciousness by which we know it is His chit, and the self that we cannot but affirm ourselves to be is His ânanda. Each one of us is in that pillar of light, no matter where he may move in the space of being, nor where he may go in the time of consciousness. And no man will ever escape these three realities: he cannot say: "I am not"; he cannot say: "I am unconscious"; nor can he at last fail to rest his knowledge upon the outer world of being. Though there be millions of worlds within worlds and beings within beings, sat, chit and ânanda are everywhere present, and everywhere in one. The things that we see and touch and taste and smell and hear are sat, true being, and in that realm of being no man will ever escape from that upon which all rely, the evidence of their senses, even though his clairvoyance may extend through all possible planes up the pillar of light.

God the Universe, the Sachchidânanda Brahman, is not *composed* of three realities put together—sat, chit and ânanda—but That[1] spreads itself out in space and time, in what is called manifestation, where and when the qualities of sat and chit come into activity amid the mysterious cyclic changes that go on in the life of the eternal super-being.

We find ourselves in such a dual world of matter and consciousness, the great passive and active principles. In the seventh chapter of *The Bhagavad-Gîtâ* Shrî Krishna says: " Earth, water, fire, air, ether, manas, buddhi and ahamkâra —these are the eightfold division of My manifestation." The last word is prakriti, translated variously as " matter " and as " nature," but manifestation expresses the idea of it, as the word comes from kri, " to make or do," with the preposition pra, which means " forth ". It may strike some students as strange that these eight manifestations should be mentioned together as though they formed one class, and should be described in the next verse as " My lower manifestation ". There is a good reason for that, however, for they are in one class, although they fall into two subdivisions within it, composed of the first five and the last three respectively. The first five words name the five planes of human evolution—earth is the physical plane, water the astral, fire the mental, air the buddhic, and ether the âtmic or nirvânic. The Sanskrit word which is here translated ether is âkâsha, and this is regarded

[1] We need here a new pronoun. English writers have long been feeling the necessity of one that will comprise both he and she, and yet be singular in number; but here we want one to include the sense of " it " as well.

as the root-matter of the five planes under consideration.
These five planes must be regarded for our present purpose in
one eyeful, if I may use such an expression, as one world
having five degrees or grades of density in its matter; we
must disregard the steps which these degrees of density make,
and think of the whole as one world shading imperceptibly
downwards, from the highest point to the lowest.

The remaining three divisions of " My manifestation "
are manas, buddhi and ahamkâra. Here we have the âtma-
buddhi-manas familiar to Theosophists. They are three
faculties or powers of consciousness. Ahamkâra means literally " I-making," and agrees with the Theosophical conception
of âtmâ. Manas is the faculty with which consciousness
cognises the material aspect of the world ; buddhi is that with
which it becomes aware of the consciousness within that
world, and ahamkâra or âtmâ is that with which it individual-
ises these experiences and so makes for each of us " *my*
world " and " *my* consciousness ". This last faculty knows
the one I, but it manifests it in a thousand or a million
apparent I's.

When Shrî Krishna throws consciousness and matter
into the same class, he does not suggest that consciousness
is in any way superior to matter or above it. We are not to
think that consciousness is manifested in a fivefold world
from above that world ; matter and consciousness are equal
partners, two aspects of one manifestation. It is not that
life or consciousness manifests in the material world from
above with different degrees of power. The world is just as
much a world of life as of matter ; the two are mixed
together, and on the whole equally.

To understand this, consider the following. In the physical level of the world we seem to be in a world of matter.
The matter is so obvious, so prominent, so dominant, so ever-
present, that we have some difficulty in recognising the

existence of any life at all in this plane, and even then we find only sparks or points of it embodied in men, animals and other beings. It looks very much like a great world of matter in which only a tiny bit of life incarnates. When one enters on the astral plane one finds a change from this state ; there the matter is a little less dominant and the life a little more evident—the powers of consciousness are more influential and the limitations of matter less rigid, obstructive and resistive. At the next level, the lower mental, life is a degree more prominent still, and matter yet less dominant. Thus the three planes, physical, astral and lower mental, constitute a region in which we may say there is more matter than life.

Now consider the highest of the five planes. Here the conditions are quite the reverse of those in the physical world. It is a great unresting sea of the powers of consciousness. When the initiate of the fourth degree enters that plane for the first time he cannot immediately discover any matter or form at all. It is as difficult to find matter there as it is to find consciousness in the physical plane. Some evidence of this is to be seen in the attempt to describe the nirvânic plane which was made by Bishop Leadbeater in his article on the subject in *The Inner Life*. In the comparison that we have been making the buddhic plane may be said to offer reverse conditions to those which prevail on the astral, and the higher mental to those of the lower mental.

Suppose, then, that a visitor from some other state of being should enter our fivefold field of manifestation. If he happened to come into it at the physical level he would describe it as a world of matter in which there are points of life, centres of consciousness ; but if he touched it at its âtmic or nirvânic level he would call it a world of consciousness in which there are some points of matter.

These principles are shown in the following diagram:

GOD THE UNIVERSE		
BRAHMA : SAT (The World of Things—Earth, Water, Fire, Air, Ether)	VISHNU : CHIT (The World of Consciousness— Atma, Buddhi, Manas)	SHIVA : ANANDA (The Self, Real Life)
THE SEVEN PRINCIPLES		
Tamas (Matter) 7 — Rajas (Natural energy) 6 — Sattva (Natural law) 5 — Kriyâ (Manas) 3 — Jnâna (Buddhi) 2 — Ichchhâ (Atma.) 1	4	Represented by Mâyâ

CHAPTER II

CONSCIOUSNESS

IN Hindu and Theosophical books the terms ichchhâ, jnâna, and kriyâ are employed to indicate the three essential constituents of consciousness. Those words are usually and quite accurately translated as will, wisdom and activity, but the significance of the English words in this connection will *not* be understood unless it is clearly realised that they refer to states of consciousness and nothing else.

The three states of consciousness link the being who has them to the three great worlds—ichchhâ or will to the self, jnâna or wisdom to the world of consciousness itself, and kriyâ or activity to the world of things or being. Therefore jnâna is the very essence of consciousness.

When we see the great scope of these three states we may realise the inadequacy of their English names, which in fact draw attention principally to the positive or outward-working aspect of each of them. Consciousness is ever two-fold—as being receptive or aware, and as being active and influential, or, in other words, as possessing faculties and powers. Each of its three states is both a faculty and a power.

Ichchhâ is our consciousness of self, and also the power that is will. Jnâna is our consciousness of others, and also

2

the power that is love. And kriyâ is our consciousness of things, and also the power that is thought.

Consciousness can never be seen on any plane with any sort of clairvoyance; only being can be seen—but consciousness can be experienced, and is of course being experienced by every conscious being. Let us realise that however splendid amid the relativity of things may be the being aspect of a jivâtmâ or living self on the higher planes, it still belongs to the world of things or sat. Again, consciousness is not subject at any time or on any plane to the limitations of sat, or, to express the same fact in another way, which is not without danger of causing misapprehension, it can be and is everywhere at once, and to go from one place to another it need not cross intervening space. It crosses only time. If, for example, I ask you to walk from one place to another, and after you have done it I question: "What were you doing? Were you moving?" I should expect the answer: "No, I was not moving." And if I press the matter further and question: "What then were you doing?" I should expect the reply: "I was thinking; I was perceiving the motion of the body."

It is only by inference from observation through the senses that human beings know the position and motion of their own bodies. If you are sleeping in a Pullman berth on the railway, and the train is running smoothly, you cannot tell whether you are going head or feet first; but when you let up the blind and look at the lights and shadowy objects flitting by, you *infer* that you go head first, and then invest the body with the supposed sensations of motion in that direction.

When this freedom from space limitations that is enjoyed by consciousness is understood and remembered, it is possible to obtain accurate ideas of the nature of will, wisdom and activity as conscious operations.

CHIT OR CONSCIOUSNESS		
FORM	AWARENESS OF :	ACTS AS :
Ichchhâ	Self	Will-power
Jnâna	Others	Love-power
Kriyâ	Things or objects	Thought-power

When men speak of God they do not, as a rule, think of the Universal God of whom I have spoken, but imagine One who is the supreme consciousness of our solar system. He is one consciousness and it is that in which we all take part— not that it is divided among us, but that we share in it with Him. That great consciousness, called by Theosophists the solar Logos, shows the three powers of will, wisdom and activity. He is of Vishnu in essence, but His will puts Him in touch with Shiva and His activity with Brahmâ. But by analogy these aspects of that Vishnu have been called also Shiva, Vishnu and Brahmâ. Though these personifications are misleading, I mention them because I want to tell the story of our Vishnu's creation of His world.

First of all Brahmâ was sent forth to wield the creative power or divine activity. It is recounted in the books for the understanding of men that He performed His work by sitting in meditation, and that as He meditated the worlds took form under the power of His thought. Such was His *activity*. It was Vishnu who then entered into the material world and filled it with life, and Shiva with His power that is Self who was there as its super-being.

The true Brahmâ is outside consciousness, but this Brahmâ is not, being only a personification of the kriyâ of our solar Logos. I tell the story only to show that the creative activity was not action with hands and feet in space, but what we call thought. The matter of space in the world of sat is touched by the power of kriyâ, and takes form under its influence.

THE UNIVERSAL GOD		
BRAHMA (Being)	VISHNU (Consciousness)	SHIVA (Happiness)
	SOLAR LOGOS	
	Secondary Brahmâ (Solar Kriyâ) · Secondary Vishnu (Solar Jnâna) · Secondary Shiva (Solar Ichchhâ)	

CHAPTER III

THOUGHT-POWER

WHAT is true of the three powers of consciousness of Vishnu is true of those of any man, for all our powers are part of that great consciousness—just as the materials of our bodies, with their properties, are taken from the great sea of material being. It is the thought in any person that is his *activity* as a *man*. This activity is twofold, whether you consider the universal or the apparently particular being. (1) It is to be found in the faculty of discrimination that is behind all perception. No man passively perceives. There is no such thing as the passive reception of modifications in consciousness, and all perception is rather of the nature of looking out of a window to see what passes by. The things of the world will never break in upon anybody's consciousness. But consciousness, when it is active, opens itself to the perception of things, and thus has what, if we are very careful, we may be permitted to call a negative aspect. (2) It also acts in a positive manner, so that every thought carries with it the power over things that the thought of the solar Brahmâ exerted in the beginning. This truth about the activity of consciousness as distinct from the action of matter solves the problem of action and inaction which troubles so many students of *The Bhagavad-Gîtâ*.

In the Western world there is most dire confusion about the relation between will and desire, and much discussion as to which of these works the body and thus causes its actions in the world. The answer to that problem is that neither will nor desire directly operates the body. Thought or kriyâ is the only power that deals with things, and it is with thought-power, kriyâshakti, that the body has been built and that all its activities that are not reflex are performed. In illustration of this I will observe that whenever you pick up your pen from the table, you do it by thought-power. Lookers-on might say that they saw you pick up the pen with your hand, but it was the thought that lifted the hand. There has been a glimpse of the truth about this matter thrown into European psychology in the theory that Monsieur Emil Coué has put forward, that whenever there is a conflict in the human mind between will and thought[1] it is always thought that wins the day. That is true if we remember that we are thinking of results in action in the world, and also if we take care to observe that in the statement the term " will " is wrongly used. The theory is true, but its expression in English is clumsy.

Many illustrations may be given to make the idea vivid and impressive. One of the best gives the experience of a certain motor-car dealer in Los Angeles, whose custom it was to teach his clients how to drive the cars that they

[1] It has been pointed out that the word " imagination " is often used in this connection. When it is so used, however, it means an image in the mind—that is, a settled thought, a stepping-stone in the process of thought. Thought is like walking. You put a foot down and rest it on the ground. Then you swing your body along, with that foot as a point of application for the forces of the body against the earth. At the end of the movement you bring down the other foot ; and then you relieve the first one, poising the body in motion on the new pivot. Transition and poise thus alternate in thought. The thought-image is a poise—a thought or idea ; the transition from it to another is thinking, when the process is logical. How the imagination-process differs from the thought-process is explained in Chapter XIV. A distinction must be drawn between imagination as a process, and the production and power of mental images.

bought from him. There was a certain man, who had purchased a car and was learning to drive, but for a long time had been falling short of complete success, because of a mania for telegraph poles that is not altogether uncommon in those circumstances. This gentleman would go out in the early morning on the best road that he could find, when there was nobody about, and he would be coming along, driving his car in a tentative and unsteady manner, with his eyes on the road, and for a time blissfully ignorant of the existence of telegraph poles. Sooner or later, however, one would catch his eye, perhaps as he came to a bend in the road, and then he would begin to say to himself : " Oh, I do hope that I shall not run into that pole. I really must not run into it," and as he repeated these words the thought of the pole would become bigger and bigger in his mind, until it occupied his imagination and left little or no room for the thought of the road. Then became apparent the power of thought, for the thing that occupied his imagination, that filled his mind, dominated his action, although he was fervently wishing not to run into the post. His hands, uncertain before, now became steady upon the steering wheel, and he would find himself driving with the precision of an expert straight for the dreaded telegraph pole ; and lucky for him it was that he had a teacher by his side, for it is somewhat doubtful whether on all such occasions he could have found the presence of mind to stop his car before running off the road.

The power over the body of a steady and clear mental picture is well shown in this example, and it can be employed to restore the body to health or to help to keep it in that condition, as Monsieur Coué claims. It is also constantly effective in many other ways that people do not usually notice. Mr. Clarence Underwood, the well-known American commercial artist, and painter of the " school girl complexion " pictures for a famous brand of soap, tells how thought-power moulded the face and form of his little daughter. " Many years ago," he says, " I suddenly stopped painting the blonde woman who had dominated my work, and began to draw a girl. People asked me who she was, and I truly could not tell them. She was certainly not the model that I was using, nor any combination of several models. She was herself, and to me, at least, an ideal type. My little daughter, Valerie, was then six years old, and she loved that dark girl intensely. She would come into the studio, and stand behind my chair, and watch me paint, until discovered and dragged protestingly away. For years I drew that one face with little variation. When Valerie was a young lady, some fifteen years later, she was the living image of that pictured face which I had drawn so many years before. I know that her love and admiration for those pictures were responsible for it. Old friends of mine, when they met my daughter, would exclaim at the resemblance, although at the time when I painted the pictures Valerie was nothing but a baby, with no more semblance to the face on the canvas than I myself had. Her actual looks were changed to conform with the pictured face which she loved, and this same result may happen to any girl. The American girl of to-day is more nearly the result of the artist's ideal than she herself can possibly know."

Belief in this power is now very widespread in America, and it is no wonder that several of the famous artists of that country consider that in producing beautiful pictures of the human face and form they are playing a prominent part in the rapid development of a splendid new nation. Their pictures are well printed, and circulated by hundreds of millions in the magazines, and on the beautiful bill-boards of the country—for beauty has won a real and lasting place in American commerce. The young people of both sexes, and often the older ones as well, look at those pictures, and long "to be like that ". Mr. Harrison Fisher says that when a young girl strongly admires a type of beauty that she has seen, she unconsciously forms herself by her thinking of it into some semblance of the pictured face, and that this is a proved effect which every artist has observed. Mr. Howard Chandler Christy, whose opinion is constantly sought in the beauty contests of America, maintains that the women of that land have in a short time grown inches taller than before, largely because of the illustrations that have so depicted them, and have thus placed that physical ideal before the nation. What is constantly before the eyes tends to impress the mind, and this in turn affects the body ; and in this effect also lies the reason why husband and wife grow to resemble one another as the years go by.

Very similar to these effects is that of the pre-natal influence of a mother's thought, when it is strong and not changeable. This was an idea of the old Greek mothers, who used to contemplate the statues in order to make their children beautiful. Mrs. Ruth J. Wild, of Brooklyn, whose daughter was a prize winner in a contest in which she had to compete with many other beautiful girls, tells how during a time of great material and emotional difficulty, when she was left alone in the world, she determined that her baby should be a beautiful girl. She frequented the Brooklyn museum, and used to sit looking at the statues of Venus and Adonis. She carried with her also a magazine cover, depicting a head by the artist Boileau, and constantly pictured in her mind the beautiful daughter that was to be. When the child did come it was a girl, and, said Mrs. Wild: "All that I had dreamed about and hoped for had been built into the most beautiful child in all the world. The doctors said that they had never seen any baby like her, and one of them, knowing that I was still in destitute circumstances, offered me twenty thousand dollars for the baby. All the money in the world could not have bought her, however, for I knew that I had

3

18

succeeded. Looking into her little face I could see that it was the image of the Boileau painting, and I knew then that her figure would develop along the lines of beauty of my statues. Her figure has developed along those lines, and to this day she has the same bright-colored hair, the same dark eyelashes and, when her face is in repose, the exact expression of my Boileau picture, that I carried about so long and looked at so earnestly."

Another case is that of Mrs. Virginia Knapp, of New York. Her daughter Dorothy was chosen prize Venus of America at a beauty contest held in Madison Square Garden. This mother also set her mind on beautiful things. She would wander alone among the beauties of nature, and plead with nature to give some of her loveliness to her daughter, and she ascribes her daughter's beauty not to heredity, but to her own will and determination in pre-natal days. In these cases there is the direct influence of thought on the sensitive body of the growing infant, for it is well-known that there is no nervous connection between mother and unborn child.

That thought can affect the minds of others even at a distance, and also leave its impression on physical matter, are facts thoroughly proved, and I can bear witness to having seen this effect produced hundreds of times with perfect accuracy and often under test conditions in India and elsewhere.

I need not dwell upon the more familiar activities of thought that govern our daily lives and make our material environment highly civilised. Every department of human achievement and culture comes within its power—philosophy, the drama, science, religion and art; all applied to the smallest details of daily life. "Everything," said Emerson, "is fluid to thought." Truly in course of time men will with its power solve more of the problems of life and nature, and bring still greater forces into human service, let us hope with an ever-increasing devotion to human brotherhood, turned to an ever-advancing realisation of the spiritual purpose of human life.

CHAPTER IV

LOVE-POWER

As kriyâ, thought, is used for gaining knowledge about material things and their relationships, and is also the creative power in material life, so jnâna acquaints us with the consciousness in living things and exerts the great power of love upon and among them. Jnâna is wisdom, which is very different from knowledge. The books rightly say that all our knowledge about things is avidyâ, ajnâna, but those terms have both been translated ignorance, when they ought to have been translated unwisdom. Avidyâ carries this somewhat reprehensible significance only when reference is made to knowledge by itself, not linked with jnâna. Jnâna-vijnâna-sahita, that is wisdom together with knowledge, is the true wisdom that will lead humanity to perfection, for directed by wisdom all knowledge becomes profitable to the inner self.

Shrî Krishna made the meaning of wisdom perfectly clear in two verses in the *Gîtâ* ; when he was speaking of the possessions that men can use in the service of God for the benefit of mankind. He said:

Better than the sacrifice of any material object is the offering of wisdom, because all works without exception at last build up only wisdom. If you would realise this you must reverence the divine in all things, try to understand, and practise service. Then the wise ones who see the truth will direct you to wisdom.

Surely he was pointing out that all the work that men
have done in the world in the long course of history has perish-
ed into dust, but that the fruit of that work nevertheless exists
as wisdom in the human soul, and also that that wisdom is no
mere knowledge of things, to be accumulated by thought, but
is the realisation of life.   The distinction between a wise man
and a man of knowledge is clear, whatever may be the
department of his work in the world.   If he is a statesman
or a teacher, for example, he will not have some preconceived
idea or plan to which he will try to compel the people or the
children to submit themselves, but he will be highly sensitive
to the living conditions of those with whom he has to
deal—to their thoughts and feelings and the state of their
consciousness—and he will respect those things as much as
the engineer respects the properties of steel and timber in
his plans.   It is not the man who knows the most about a
subject who can best teach it, but the one who is sensitive to
life, and is therefore able to realise the consciousness of his
pupils.   For that he needs something more than knowledge
gained by study ; he requires experience of the heart,
springing from sympathy, and contact of life with life.   Who
is wiser in all the world than the mother who unconsciously
places her little child's happiness before all else ? Wisdom is
therefore a kind of sublimated feeling ; or rather it is a sublime
feeling, because it is essential in the soul, not transmuted
from something else below.   It has what with caution might
be described its negative aspect in sympathy or sensitiveness to others' life, and its positive form is the power of love.

It is this wisdom that is the real human feeling, and its
corruption is desire.   Wisdom is love of living beings, of life ;
but desire is love of things.   If a man is full of desire for
great material possessions or power or fame in the world,
there is still, behind all that, the longing for greater life.   But
as he makes the mistake of thinking of himself as a material

thing, merely as a body with a set of thoughts and feelings attached to it, his notion of increased life leads him solely to the enlargement of his bodily possessions and power, and he is unconscious of the fact that his neighbors are living beings—to him they are nothing more than animate complex material mechanisms, and he only thinks of them with liking or disliking as they fit in with or obstruct his own desires and plans. But the wise man is sensitive to life in those other beings. He feels it on the instant and can make no plans without taking it into consideration, and the love that thus fills his life enlarges it without any grasping on his part. For him the pursuit of fame is not possible; he is not anxious to occupy the minds of others with thoughts of himself, that he may be enlarged and multiplied in them; rather would he fill his own mind and life with them and their interests and needs, through his own universal sympathy.

Love introduces us to life, not only physically, leading to our birth in this world; but also every moment of our lives it opens us up in ready sensitiveness and leads us to new experience and duty. Every one has a picture in mind of the old-fashioned miser, who used to go down into his cellar or up to his garret, candle in hand, and lock himself in to gloat over his treasure, to pour his gold and jewels over neck and arms, and bathe in them with morbid pleasure. And yet it was no pleasure, for the man was always full of fear, jumping at every moving shadow cast by his flickering candle, starting at every sound; and it was literally true that that man's selfishness brought with it a shrinking from contact with others, a terrible narrowing of his life. But love expands and casts out fear, and makes man man. It is the real human feeling, and when men lose it they have lost their very lives, though their bodies may be moving about.

A story that is sometimes heard in India shows how different is love from thought and how the dictates of love must be followed where human life is concerned. It is told about an old man who lived in a large village in India a long time ago. He was the richest man there by far, and very powerful, but not a man of good disposition ; in fact he made it his business to use all his power and wealth to persecute and torment anyone whom he did not like, and he was therefore a terror to the villagers. This old man had a son who was kindness itself, and everybody was longing for the day when he should inherit the old man's wealth and position, and live as a blessing to all the people. A third person in this story was a wandering sannyâsî who, as he went about doing good, happened to come to this village and stay awhile. Very soon he became aware of what was going on there, and a curious temptation came into his mind, and he found himself saying : "Why should I not kill that old man, and release these people from their misery, and give the young man his opportunity to do the widespread good that he surely will do when he can ? The old man is not happy, and it does not matter what becomes of me so long as I do good." And then the question is put : "What would you do under those circumstances ? " Logic seems to say that this idea is good. But most people fortunately would do as the sannyâsî did, and let the old man live, as the heart dictates.

The wisdom in us knows that we are all one, and it could no more think that happiness could be purchased for anyone by injury to another than the mind could propose to win truth by deliberate falsity of thought. A similar problem there is before the Western world at the present day in connection with the experimentation on living animals that is going on all the time. No one likes it ; every heart shrinks from its horror, and the students who take it up in the beginning shudder at what they have to do, until the heart becomes hardened. It is all done in the name of logic and human welfare ; the mind seems to say that it is quite justifiable in order to reduce human pain. But even if it did reduce human pain, as is utterly impossible by such means while karma rules the world, it would at the same time harden human hearts and delay the progress of the race. Surely everybody thinks of humanity of the future as composed of people full of great love and power, not creeping about in the cracks of the earth in wretched servitude to decrepit bodies that must be sustained at the expense of incredible pain to their fellow-beings ; and yet they do not seem to realise that their unwisdom puts off those glorious days.

Wisdom is seen also in simple sentiment like that of the philosopher Emerson who, when he returned home from a journey, used to shake hands with the lower branches of his trees, and say that he could feel that they were pleased to have him back again, as he was to be among them ; and the same thing is apparent in very much of the writing and poetry of Dr. Rabindranath Tagore, who can enter into the spirit of a little child or of a stream, and sense the purposes of life also in the squalid streets of a crowded town. Jnâna, wisdom, is love, consciousness of the same kind of life in all.

CHAPTER V

WILL-POWER

LET us recall the experience of the man of Los Angeles who could not learn to drive his car because his thought of the telegraph poles would persist, despite all his efforts to the contrary, in directing his hands. Though the power of thought is shown in that illustration, do not imagine that it exhibits also the relative feebleness of will. The will was not defeated; it was in abeyance. The man was not willing—he was wishing; and there is all the difference in the world between those two things. The presence of a wish or a hope in the human mind indicates the absence of will, and the person who gives himself up to wishing surrenders for the time being his divinity and abdicates his throne.

The utter separateness and mutual exclusiveness of wishing and willing can be shown in a very simple way. If your pencil is lying on the table, and you consider the question as to whether you will pick it up or not, you will come to the conclusion: "I will pick it up," or else to the decision: "I will not pick it up." There will be no wishing at all about the matter, because you are quite confident that it lies within your power. But if the pencil weighed half a ton, or if you happened to think that it did so, you might then find yourself saying: "Oh, I *do* wish that I could lift up that pencil!"

4

The man who wishes acknowledges thereby his dependence upon external chance ; he is in a waiting state, and not waiting willingly for something that he knows is sure to come in its appointed time, but just hoping that the world will do something that he happens to desire. It is impossible to overestimate the foolishness of wishing or the utter abnegation of will that it involves. and it may be said incidentally that only the man who is willing to give it up completely and for ever can proceed far on the occult path.

What then is the will, if thought is the power that works among things ? It is the power that works among thoughts and feelings. It is concentration. It is attention. It is the power that subdivides the mind into the conscious and the subconscious. If the man in the motor-car had known this simple truth, he could have dismissed his fear of the telegraph poles very easily. He would have said to himself : " Stop thinking about that pole. Fix your eye upon the road, and think about that. Forget the pole by filling your mind with the thought of the road along which you want to go." If he had tried to control his thought, instead of his hands, all would have been well. The same thing has surely been observed by very many inexperienced drivers at night, when a car with glaring head-lights is about to pass in the opposite direction ; it is then necessary for the driver not to allow himself to be fascinated with the idea that is born of the fear of those advancing lights, but to turn his mind away from them and fix it on the darkness of the road along which he wants to go, although he cannot see it.

Wishing is no form of will ; but just an enlargement of desire ; while desire is usually the wish to possess something that one has not, wishing covers the entire field, and brings with it a multitude of fears for the loss of what one has, or about the many chances that may thwart the satisfaction of desire. It is not so much a reflection of will as a reflection of love, but love distorted beyond all semblance, because it has become attached to things, whereas its proper sphere is conscious life.

Will is thus the âtmâ, the self, realising itself, and exhibiting its power over all its own relations to the world of life and things. The will is the self being itself, and its nature can be discerned as this whenever men try to determine their own future. It is connected with the verb " to be," not with the verb " to do ". When a man determines : " I will work hard in my business and make a lot of money," he is really saying to himself, almost subconsciously : " I will be rich," and that works itself into his thought and keeps it in service to this mood of his being, and then the thought directs the work.

When a man acts from within without full knowledge of the consequences he acts from what he *is*, not from what he thinks, and thus the will is in operation. And since no man thinks out fully the consequences of his action before he acts, in every piece of human work there is some will. An extreme measure of this is seen when a person wills to do a thing without knowing at all how to do it. Then he who wills the end wills the means, for he is declaring the power of the Self within. He is performing a splendid act of concentration, focusing all the powers of his heart and mind in one direction, and this concentration finally produces the result. The man who knows that he is master of his own consciousness sufficiently to produce this concentration can will when others cannot.

The will leads ultimately to real super-conscious life, happiness, ânanda. The ânanda state of being is timeless ; but consciousness moves in time (though not in space), and as it does so it produces evolution or unfoldment, which, however, is not progress. This is a difficult matter, which I will deal with in Chapter XXI, but here it must be noted

that it introduces the principle of obscuration into consciousness and divides the mind, as the will is directing the whole
of itself to a part of itself to realise that part more perfectly
for a time. It is just as a child at school might go into the
music room, and there give all his attention to music for a
period, and forget all about the very existence of such matters
as geography and history ; indeed, the more perfect that
forgetfulness the better will be the music. That process is
necessary while something new is being acquired. It makes
the subconscious mind, in which will, wisdom and activity
are going on all the time unperceived by the conscious mind
—or rather, by the conscious part of the mind, because there
are not two minds.

To make this point clearer I will recount an experience
that I had in a South Indian town with an old gentleman
who was expert in wielding the powers of the mind. Among
the many interesting experiments that he showed me was one
with a pack of cards. First he wrote something on a piece of
paper, and folded it up and gave it to me to put in my pocket.
Then he told me to shuffle the cards and spread them face
downwards on the platform on which I was sitting in the
Indian style. When this had been done he told me to
pick up any card I liked, so quite casually I let my hand
drop on one of them and lifted it up. "Now," said he,
"look at the card, and also at the paper which I gave you."
I did so, and when I unfolded the paper I found written upon
it the name of the card that I had picked up. At the old
gentleman's request I then handed the cards to two Hindu
friends who had accompanied me to his dwelling, and then
he repeated the experiment twice more, having given a
new paper to each of them, and without touching the cards
himself.

It then occurred to me to try a little experiment on my
own account, so I requested him to give me a new paper and

try again, which he was perfectly willing to do, as he was interested not merely in showing his powers but in instructing me with regard to them as far as that was possible. I shuffled the cards and spread them as before, but this time as I was about to pick one up I fixed my mind upon his and addressed him silently, saying: " Now, whatever card you have chosen, I will *not* have that card." Then I picked up one of the cards, took out the paper and unfolded it, and found that this time the two did not agree, and no one could have been more visibly astonished than the old gentleman when I held up the paper and the card together for his inspection. He had apparently never before failed. Thereupon I told him what I had done, and he said that that perfectly explained the matter and he would tell me how he performed the experiment.

"First," he said, " I decide upon a particular card and write down its name. Then I concentrate upon it steadily and transfer the thought to your mind, where under these conditions it is also held very steady, though without your conscious knowledge. Now, the subconscious mind has its own powers of perception, and when properly directed it is quite capable of seeing what is on the underside of those cards although the physical eye cannot do so ; and further, that image in the mind next directs the hand and arm to the exact spot where the card is lying. But when you set your will against mine you must have destroyed the image that I made." In his Oriental way he complimented me on the strength of my will, but it is quite possible that had he been forewarned of my intention he could have carried out the experiment successfully all the same, as was indeed the case with my two Hindu friends immediately afterwards, when they tried not to pick up the chosen card but were literally compelled to do so every time. It may be suggested that the old gentleman ought by thought-transference to have been aware of what I was doing, but I think he was too intent upon his own part in the experiment to notice it.

Later on, I had a surprising continuation of this experience, which occurred in my own College at Hyderabad in the Province of Sind, two thousand miles away from the town of Trichinopoly, where I had spent a morning with that old gentleman. One evening, after a hard day's work, I was sitting in my room along with two friends, one of whom was a member of my staff—professor of political science. This gentleman, a Hindu who had graduated with honors from Oxford University, had picked up while in England some very clever conjuring tricks with cards, and he was that evening entertaining us with some of them for the sake of relaxation. My thought was far away from any matter of psychical research; it was rather occupied with the serious troubles of the moment connected with the political movement working among the college students, and calculated in my opinion to injure their future and the country very seriously. Suddenly, without warning, I heard a full-bodied man's voice speak right in the middle of my head. It spoke only six words: "Five of clubs; try that experiment," but somehow I knew that it referred to the experience I had had at Trichinopoly some time before. I obeyed the voice, and at once wrote down "five of clubs" on a piece of paper, folded this up, and asked my friend the professor to put it in his pocket. Next I requested him to shuffle his cards, which I had not touched at all, and to spread them face downwards on the floor on which we were sitting, and then pick one up at random, and compare it with what was written on the paper. When he turned up his card it proved to be the five of clubs, and you can imagine his surprise when he found that written upon the paper which was in his pocket. I do not know for certain how the voice directed me in this case; but knowing what I do of thought-power, I consider it quite reasonable to believe that the old gentleman living two thousand miles away had become aware of our occupation, had suggested the experiment to my mind, and had assisted in making it a success. As an exhibition of the way in which thought-power and the will may act in the subconscious part of the mind this experience was valuable.

When we are considering the way in which thought is the working power among the things of our life and in the body, we must take into account that it is sometimes subconscious thought, and that in fact very many of the so-called accidents of life are really due to our own thought-power operating in this way, often directed by the will. A man may, perhaps, on a particular evening have nothing very special to do. He decides to go out for a walk. He puts on his hat and coat, or maybe his turban, and goes out into the road, and casually decides to go this way or that way. In the course of his walk he happens to meet some-one who suggests to him a new business proposition or a new line of thought that eventually changes his fortunes or his life, so that looking back upon it he will say that that was the turning-point of his career, and will often exclaim what a lucky thing it was that he chanced to take a walk that evening, and to go along the street where he met his friend. Perhaps it was no chance, but the larger man within him may have been directing him, as surely as my hand was guided to the chosen card among the many that were spread on the platform. This at least everybody knows, that there is someone inside him who succeeds occasionally in impressing the conscious part of the mind with what is usually called the voice of conscience, which knows far more about the true direction of life than does the man working within the limits of the conscious mind.

Later on, when the learning period is over, and the man's consciousness has become more powerful, so that he is able to deal with music and history and geography all at once, the act of concentration will no longer be necessary, except as a swift power for the use of the moment. He will then have at his constant command all the powers and all the knowledge which he has acquired little by little in the midst of the obscuration caused by his concentration upon learning. Then the subconscious or unconscious mind and the conscious mind will have become one.

Let us, then, have clearly before us the true distinction between ichchhâ and kriyâ, or will and activity, and not forget that the first of these is poles asunder from any sort of wish and that the second is the activity of thought, and both are powers, the latter over things, including the body, and the former over oneself, that is to say one's own thoughts and feelings.

CHAPTER VI

MATTER, ENERGY AND LAW

WE have observed that in the world of consciousness there are always present three principles, evident in different degrees and proportions at different times. So also in the world of sat there are three principles to be discerned, called tamas, rajas and sattva, translatable as matter, energy and law. Ancient and modern scientists have equally discovered these three in that one, and have also observed their inseparability. They are principles of matter; not properties, but states, of material being, and a body can exhibit them in different degrees at different times, as consciousness can employ will, or love or thought, though all are always present to some extent.

The objective world is a world of bodies that obstruct one another, and can block consciousness as well when the latter submits to matter by immersing itself in a body. An object is seen only because it obstructs our sight, and the world is full of light only because the darkness or impenetrability to light of its material atmosphere diffuses the solar rays. Every atom of matter is thus, as it were, a dark spot in space, which is impenetrable and so can be acted upon only from the outside. The interpenetration of matter spoken of by Theosophists means only that finer bodies can exist in the interstices of coarser ones, and in such cases though two or more *bodies* interpenetrate and thus occupy the same space, the *matter* of those bodies does not actually do so. This quality of darkness or stability or resistance or

5

obstruction seen in the objects of the world was called by the ancient scientists tamas. It is that quality of matter which in common speech and thought is taken as matter itself, that which gives body to matter and so forms points in space for the application of force. Matter has thus what might be called a will of its own (though it is a negative will, stubbornness), and is unquestionably itself, and apparently quite unwilling to surrender its existence.

During the last century it was widely thought that all the world was built up of tiny bricks, called atoms, of which there was a considerable variety. Each one of these was held to be utterly unchangeable, so that it could be said that the units of matter were immortal—that is, uncreatable and indestructible. Then it was considered that just as a hundred thousand bricks might be used to build any one of many different kinds of houses, and just as, one having been built, it could be altered and refashioned by the removal and re-use of its constituent bricks ; so was the world composed of atoms constantly being re-arranged into its changing forms. For all practical human purposes the idea is true. That is an exhibition of tamas in a certain grade of material being, but it would be utterly true only if stability were the sole constituent property of the world of matter that comes within the grasp of the five senses.

The second constituent of substance is the energy of matter, rajas, which now in scientific circles is generally being thought of as the source and basis of matter itself, though time will surely show that it also is material and never without body or position. The conception of natural energy that one finds in elementary books on mechanics will serve very well to describe this constituent property of substance. It is well known to all students that no material body will change its condition of equilibrium or motion without the application to it of some form of energy, unless

it is a complex body in which the ripening of internally active
forces results in a new balance of the whole, as, for instance,
when a rock on a hill-side rots, and suddenly falls down.

A ball, for example, standing on a billiard table, will not
start moving on its own account. If it be moving, it will not
come to rest without the application of some form of resistance or other counteracting force from the outside—the
resistance of the air, the friction on the table, or obstruction
by the cushions or other balls ; and the energy of the ball in
motion and of the force which cancels that motion may be
shown to be equal.

But all these things are surface phenomena, showing
rajas as the chemical atom exhibits tamas. And as the atom
can be decomposed, and its tamas aspect attenuated until
people say it is only energy, so may energy emerge from
and fade into the background of sattva or law, which
is the very essence of the objective world, as jnâna is
that of the world of consciousness. This energy may
overstep time as consciousness oversteps space, as, for
example, if I lift up a ball from the ground on to the
table. A certain amount of energy was spent in lifting
it, and the same amount will be expressed again if at some
future time it falls from the table to the floor, as could be
ascertained if it were practicable to make it do work in falling
or to measure the heat generated by its impact with the floor.
Heat, sound, light, electric phenomena, chemical potential,
and many others are forms of energy, and so far as can
humanly or in any otherwise be discovered there is no par-
ticle of matter anywhere without some form of it. Recent
studies in connection with relativity have brought up for
reconsideration the question of the conservation of energy,
but those enquiries dig deep into the inner relationships of
the constituent properties of substance and do not vitiate the
practical reality of the principle of energy. It is sufficient

for our purpose to realise that there is natural energy, and that it is not spontaneity.

The third constituent property of matter is law. I know that this sounds strange, and that most scientific students will say offhand that the world is composed of only two things, matter and energy, and yet they will affirm that law and order are apparent everywhere. There is some inconsistency in this position, and the ancient scientists of India did not fall into it, for without hesitation they said that sattva or law was one of the properties of the material side of being. It is in fact so, and is really no more difficult a conception than the one that energy is objective. Nowhere in all the world does anybody ever find matter or energy without the exhibition of some law which determines the nature of the body's activity and its relations with other bodies. Every chemical element, every atom, has its function, just as surely as every seed has its tendency to grow and form a particular kind of plant, and the working of this law is part of the routine of nature, sat or being.

It was perfectly clear to the ancient scientists that sattva, rajas and tamas were the gunas or properties of matter, that all matter was nothing but these three, and that they could never be anything but matter. The three words are also used in an adjectival form to describe the character of things, as, for instance, in *The Bhagavad-Gîtâ*, where we read about sâttvic, tâmasic and râjasic foods, which are those which tend to build up the type of the body in which the mentioned quality is predominant, so that a râjasic body is an energetic or even restless body. Every object contains all the three gunas, but one predominates and gives it its outstanding quality, just as every consciousness or portion of chit certainly exhibits will, love and thought, although they are not equally in evidence in a given character, and one of them is usually the decided leader and inspirer of the other two.

CHAPTER VII

THE DIVINE AND THE MATERIAL

WE have now to compare the world of sat with that of chit, to see how they are related. The first is rightly called material, and the second may best be described as the divine. It must be realised that many as may seem to be the things of the material world and the consciousnesses of the world of chit, each world is still, in fact, only one thing or one consciousness, of which the many are parts.

This great truth is clearly evident among material things, and its bearing is most important. The world of being is not composed of a great many independent things all put together or synthesised; it is not built up of a great number and variety of pieces of itself or bricks. On the contrary, the process is just the reverse, and all the things that we know are nothing but abstractions from it. They are one, and their unity is shown in their utter external dependence upon one another. Consider, for example, what takes place in the child mind when it opens its eyes to the world. First of all there is just a big indefinite something there, and gradually in that general mass more prominent or vivid things begin to be distinguished, and later on, among those, the smaller things. It is something like the vision that a traveller has when his ship is nearing the shore. First, something is seen which might be land; then it becomes clearer and more strongly defined, the mountains are visible; then the voyager begins to perceive trees and houses, until, when he is very near, people and animals and even flowers can be seen.

And psychologically a similar discrimination from the block or mass of things is essential to the process of gaining knowledge ; every syllogism has its universal premise, without which there would be no reason and no acquisition of clear knowledge, which is after all never the gaining of something new, but a clear perception of what was dim or unnoticed before. It is well known that we perceive things by comparison. Put a dog and a cat together and study their resemblances and differences, and you will afterwards know what a dog is, or what a cat is, better than if you had studied it alone. Again, the best thinker on any subject is the man who has already the most ideas to compare with it, provided those ideas have been well digested and are clear and well arranged in his mind. All thinking is really abstract ; the mind cannot hold two ideas at once, but it may hold one which includes two or more, in which they are but parts of the greater whole.

It is not only logically but in fact that the smaller is dependent upon the greater or the part upon the whole. It is characteristic of material things that they have no initiative and do not change themselves, but depend upon externals for their change. Thus a book may lie on the table, and it remains there because the table is there. The table in turn is supported by the flooring planks, and those by the beams, which again rest on the walls. The walls are supported on the foundations, and the foundations on the earth. Further, the earth is a material body supported in space by the invisible strands of nature's material energy ; so it depends upon the other planets, the sun and the stars. It is only the whole of being that is self-sustaining, and all the parts depend upon that. It cannot be too emphatically affirmed that the whole is not made up of the parts, but the parts are deductions from the whole, in which they have their support and sustenance and root.

In the world of law all objective reality eternally exists. We know, for example, that when you explode together the right proportions of the two colorless gases oxygen and hydrogen, both will disappear from sight and some water will have taken their place. Certainly it will be said that the same essential matter is still there and also the same energy, but it has to be realised that you have not produced anything new even in the way of properties. It is evident that the water was not there before, and is there now, and if you were thinking only of properties or the appearances of things you might imagine that something had come out of nothing. But all that has happened is that you have made manifest to yourself and to others, who in this respect are one with you, the reality always existent.

The best simile that I can give for this is that of a child playing with picture-blocks. It has a box containing about twenty cubical blocks of wood, and on each side of each block there is a square piece of a picture. The child puts its blocks on the table or the floor, and turns them about and re-arranges them side by side until all the right pieces have been put together so as to show one picture. Then he mixes them up again and arranges them with another side upper-most, so as to form another picture. He might think that he had made those pictures, but it is not so ; there was first an artist and all that the child did was to put the things together so that the picture made by the artist should appear. So when the oxygen and hydrogen are put together does the water appear, and nothing has been added to or taken away from reality. And the same is true of everything, so that all human production and invention follows the same law. It is this reality that the mind perceives as what is usually called natural law. That law is an existent reality—sattva—the world of ideas, the objective universal mind.

Another name has sometimes been given to sat—the great passive principle. In this plenum, as I have said, there is no initiative, because there is no time, which belongs to chit. We have seen the utter dependence of the book on the table, the table on the floor, and so on, and considered the totality of things. The totality must be self-existent, self-creative, self-changing; there is no external being of its own kind to apply material energy to it from the outside. In other words it is at the same time divine. Brahmâ is cherished by Vishnu.

But chit is the divine in every part. It is the great active principle, consciousness self-existing, self-created, self-changing, independent and all-initiative, the being of time. I have for a very specific reason used the word divine instead of the term spiritual that may occur to some minds to represent the idea. The word spirit carries with it some sense of fine matter, breath-like and ethereal, but still matter. But the word divine comes from the same source as the Sanskrit "div," which means "to shine," and appears in such words as div, heaven, divâkâra, the sun, and deva, a celestial being.

The divine is thus that which shines with its own light, or from within, and many of the ancients took the sun as its symbol, because from the sun shines forth all the light and heat and life of our world; while the moon stands ever against it as the symbol of matter, shining only with reflected light. By every one who takes the trouble to think about the matter, the Divine Being, or solar Logos, is distinguishable from the material, or His world, by His character of independence and initiative. One of the most significant words describing Him is Swayambhu, the self-existent, He is the omnipotent, the omnipresent and the omniscient, because He is the whole of the chit in our solar system— chit to perfection—while man is only a part of that chit, and has the three qualities only without their prefix omni. Strictly, the word God should not be used to describe this great Consciousness, who is our Biggest Brother. Our consciousness, like our body, is something that we use, not that we are. We really belong to the Universal God, the real life, beyond matter and consciousness, beyond purusha and prakriti, beyond the material and the divine.

CHAPTER VIII

HARMONY

OUR story of the pillar of light told first of the night when Vishnu and Brahmâ were not working together in harmony, but met and quarrelled, until Shiva restored harmony by His presence, made them realise that both were one in Him, and started a new day of being. So we find that chit and sat, or in a smaller sphere man and the external world of his experience, seem to be in dire opposition, until we discover that there is utter harmony of purpose in their relations, that there is a good reason for their apparent conflict.

Ânanda is behind them both ; in Shiva they have their union. The contact of chit with sat is fraught with ânanda or happiness, as every creature evidences that loves its life, for what is commonly called life is the interplay between the two. It is a familiar thought that below the human kingdom life is full of happiness, that in the animal world pain is not frequent or lasting, and the moment of fear or dread comes only when there is the threat of life's destruction. The millions of cows that go month by month to the stockyards of Chicago and other cities have no inkling of fear or sorrow till their end draws nigh, because their knowledge and imagination do not tell them of what is in store, and out in the fields life has been sweet, though men would call it narrow. Again, in the state of nature

fear usually operates upon the glands to enhance the
physical powers, and this stimulates the consciousness, as
when a small creature enjoys the skill of the stealth with
which he avoids a bigger one.

The story has been told elsewhere of the great seal of
San Francisco. Some years ago there lived on the rocks
just off the cliffs a great seal that was king of the herd that
is still there, and within the memory and tradition of man
he had been leader for a hundred and twenty years. It
happened, however, one day that another magnificent seal,
younger and in the prime of life, arrived from the south, and
seemed to think that he ought to be the king of those rocks.
So the newcomer made battle with the old leader and the
two fought strenuously for three days, when the older one,
covered with wounds, swam to shore and died. Such is a
picture of what has been described as "nature red in tooth
and claw with ravin," but if you look at it from the standpoint
of the indwelling consciousness you will see that that battle
was not without its joy. Creatures at that level live more
in sensation than in reflection, and old age for them is not
the profitable thing that it can be for man. Indeed, when
the power of the senses of the body begins to decline, consciousness quickly follows in its wake, as it has no longer
the vivid stimulus which was its before. Therefore that the
seal's consciousness should go out from its body in a burst
of glory, amid the most vivid experience that it had ever
had, was no matter for our pity, especially as in the great
excitement of the battle it is highly improbable that the
creature was susceptible to much physical pain.

When we come to man, truly life is not all happiness,
but the reason for that is to be found in the fact that he, in
the assertion of his newly realised powers, has created
disharmony between himself and the world. It is he who
in the enjoyment of chit has overlooked ânanda, and Shiva

must be revealed to him before he can recover the child state of the animal that he has lost. In man's life, Vishnu and Brahmâ must become friends, and in their union Shiva will be there.

It is not a common thought in the Western world that harmony between human consciousness and its environment is one of the great realities of life. Even those people who do believe that this is God's world for the most part think that it is merely the place where He keeps upon probation the souls that He has made, so that after a time He may decide which are worth keeping and which ought to be thrown away as badly made. And those who believe merely in the evolution of form do not usually think that the human mind, though regarded as a product of nature, is in harmony with its source, but that it has somehow developed itself as an unwanted parasite, and is holding its place on the face of nature merely as a tenacious intruder. But the harmony is there nevertheless, and it is something most wonderful, the child of Shiva Himself; it is verily as Shiva Himself reborn to unite Vishnu and Brahmâ.

To put it in more ordinary language, I would say that nature has proved herself man's friend. It is true that the process of nature is one of decay, and that all man's handiwork is soon rased to the dust, but were it not so this world could not be God's school for man. If houses were imperishable and by some strange magic the same food could be eaten over and over again, few men would work to produce new things, and indeed the extra work required for the destruction of the old things encumbering the earth would present additional discouragement to those few who were willing to work to make something new. Man would have little incentive to use his powers of thought or will. Nature has not made life too easy for man, but on the other hand she has not made it too difficult, but has always presented to him experience of such a kind as favors the growth of conscious powers such as his. The witness to this fact is man himself, who has been growing throughout the ages and is advancing steadily into greater power in the future, through the active use of his faculties.

One of the Upanishads has a curious definition of man, where it speaks of him as the being who is both powerful and powerless, both ignorant and wise. Compare him in a state of nature with any other creature, and behold his helplessness and ignorance! He has not natural clothing, nor natural weapons worth the name, nor speed of foot or wing to escape from his enemies, nor has he the natural knowledge of instinct which tells other creatures what is food and what poison, who are friends and who enemies, and how to make a home. One might think that nature had discriminated against man, to send him thus helpless into the world; but the fact is not so. Man without natural clothing learned to use his intelligence, and in consequence has provided for himself clothing with which he can live in any climate, and through his intelligence he has learned to make weapons and tools which have crowned him master of the world.

Primitive man might have complained of his disabilities, and prayed to God for their removal; but intelligent man, who is the same one reincarnated, looks back and thanks God for the opportunities that were given to him, and for the honor that was done him, that he was ranked through the ages as a divine being, creating himself constantly by his own work, and not as a material thing moulded by force from the outside. Now he sees the harmony between man and his environment throughout all time, and realises that the world has been and is the friend of man—not a sentimental friend, but a friend in need and indeed.

Because man belongs to the divine side of things, not to the material, he unfolds in this manner, winning ever for himself a greater measure of the divine powers, and God helps him by incarnating Himself as the principle of harmony. He is omnipotent, yet there are some things that He cannot do. He cannot, for example, make a tall dwarf or a square circle, for if the man were tall he would not be a dwarf and if the form were square it would not be a circle. And so also He could not make a dependent will, for the will that was not independent would be no will at all. Hence He acknowledges man's divinity by this great arrangement for the evolution of his consciousness and its powers, whereby man is verily self-existent, self-created and divine, now and through all time.

It is this harmony between chit and sat in our world of experience that is mâyâ, often spoken of as illusion. It is illusion not because it is in any way an unreality, but because it is taken as life, and mistaken for the true life which is ânanda. Hence the books say that to be liberated man must escape even from this harmony, once the evolution of his consciousness is complete, must destroy what is sometimes called the junction of the seer and the seen, and remain thereafter residing in his own state. That state is ânanda, and is also kaivalya, the state of oneness, for the unity of Shiva is never disturbed even by the presence of Vishnu and Brahmâ.

In *The Bhagavad-Gîtâ* Shrî Krishna speaks of this harmony also as his daivîprakriti. In common speech the word *life* is accurately used to represent the interplay that is mâyâ, when people think of life not as the chit inside them, nor as the energy of nature outside, but as this harmonious interaction between the two, in which both the inner and the outer are taken into consideration. As soon as one writes philosophy people think that something new is necessarily meant by such words as life, but in this case at all events it is not so. That life is a mâyâ, an illusion, only because it is not the true life that is happiness, the life of Shiva Himself, but is only His rebirth—the reflection of His oneness—in this duality.

The same great truths are spoken of again in the *Gîtâ* (Chapter 8), where Shrî Krishna tells of the four great divisions of reality, adhyâtmâ, adhidaiva, adhibhûta and adhiyajna. The first of these is Shiva, beyond the eightfold manifestation. The second and third are the great active and passive principles, the divine and the material, like "twins upon a line" (to use an expression employed in *The Voice of the Silence* for a different purpose). The fourth relates to "Me here in the body"; it is the principle of sacrifice, whereby life (the interplay between chit and sat) is made holy. *Sacrifico* in Latin means "I make holy"; sacrifice is seen in the world in the way in which consciousness and matter minister to each other in what we call life, and that in which one creature is always yielding up something to another, either involuntarily or voluntarily, so that all become one organised whole, and thus are holy.

There is no motion without this sacrifice; that is why it has been said that God is motion. Another way in which the lower three of the four are to be seen is in the forms of space, time and motion. Space is connected with the material side of things, time with consciousness, and motion is the representative of Deity, the adhyâtmâ. Some old Sophists propounded an amusing argument to the effect that no object could ever move, for, they said: "It cannot move in the space where it is, and certainly it cannot move in the space where it is not." Of course, if there were nothing but matter it could not move. But we know that an object can move *from* the place where it is *to* some other place where before it was not. This translation implies the existence of a principle transcending the limitations of space. Space is a limitation; it is only a part of reality, less than the whole. In it, motion represents divinity.

In studying consciousness a similar difficulty is found. People often wonder how it is possible for them to be the same conscious beings that they were yesterday, or a year ago, or in childhood, or in previous lives. How, they wonder, can that consciousness, which is a changing thing, be both what it was and what it now is ? It is because the principle of motion is above and beyond time, which is the limitation of consciousness. Space belongs to the passive principle ; time belongs to the active principle ; and motion represents God or Shiva.

We have in our composition not only matter in the form of bodies limited in space, and consciousness, with its three powers limited by time ; we have also God, never absent, always transcending these limitations of time and space. This God in us, who is one in all, we call "I." That is why Shrî Krishna always says that the man who has attained perfection, who has realised the truth, "will come unto Me." When Shrî Krishna says "I" he means also the "I" in the person whom he is addressing. There is only one "I," and the man who finds it in himself will know it in all.

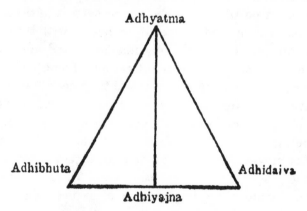

CHAPTER IX

THE SEVEN PRINCIPLES

NOW, inasmuch as there are three aspects of consciousness, and three constituents of material being, and the harmony between them which is mâyâ, there are seven fundamental realities, no more nor less, in all the world of man's experience. Those seven are not derived from three in our system of mâyâ or life, because it is only part of a bigger system in which the seven already existed; but in making His trinity out of His sevenfold self, Shiva lends, as it were, three of the seven to Brahmâ and three more to Vishnu. keeping the seventh, ânanda, for Himself.

It will be seen from this that these seven are perfectly equal, and none of them is made up of a mixture or combination of any of the others, and they are rightly called principles —first things. If for purposes of convenience we represent them by numbers, those numbers are only arbitrary names, and do not give the realities any relative position ; or, if we represent them by diagrams, that is only for mnemonic purposes, and the mathematical properties of the diagrams should not be ascribed to the principles. The danger of using such diagrams is that they themselves belong to one principle, and tend to cause the others to be seen from the standpoint of that one, and thus obscure their real nature.

The first diagram requires little explanation, as it shows the interlaced triangles familiar to Theosophists. It is the best indication of the seven, and I have put numbers to name them—1, 2, 3, 4, 5, 6, 7. The upward-pointing triangle is chit, and the downward pointing one is sat, and the whole is a

7

symbol of the expression through two related trinities of seven
equal principles, which may be called the seven principles of
God, and are tabulated beneath the diagram.

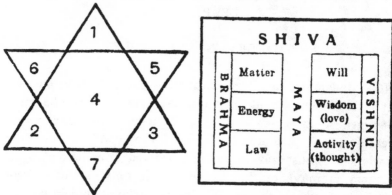

The second diagram shows how these seven are distribut-
ed in the great trinity; but the student must take care
especially in this case not to think of one set as above
another set in space.

Principles	Qualities of God and Ideals of Men
1. Ichchhâ	Freedom
2. Jnâna	Unity
3. Kriyâ	Comprehension
4. Mâyâ	Harmony
5. Sattwa	Truth
6. Rajas	Goodness
7. Tamas	Beauty

On the long road to happiness every one goes through
three steps in his evolution—first, the stage of sat, then
that of chit, and finally ânanda. This indicates why all beings

seek happiness, and all the seven principles which actuate their lives in the world are but means to that end. Even love, the very essence of consciousness, disappears in that.

Man being, in his present phase, in the chit aspect, thinks of God in nature, or sat, as outside himself, and of God in consciousness, or chit, as within himself, but He is equally present in both, and in practice men seek their happiness in both these spheres, that is to say, some seek what seem to them the greatest things in life by " retreating within," and others pursue what appear to them the true ends of life by " advancing boldly without ". Every one is more fundamentally eager to reach one of the seven ideals than the other six. The principles of God tabulated above thus become the ideals of man. Yet as each man belongs to Shiva, he has, like Him, all the seven principles at work putting his consciousness in touch with all the seven fundamental realities of life. Still, unlike Shiva, he has them unequally, and always one is stronger than the rest. That one is called his ray. All the universal principles are always exerting their attraction upon all men, but each man responds principally to that of his own ray, which then becomes his greatest ideal in life, and can stir his consciousness into the most vivid life of which he is capable.

Ichchhâ is will and, from the discussion we have already had about it, it is clear that the state of life of the being who enjoys it is one of freedom. When this principle is the strongest in a man, he will value freedom above everything else. Jnâna, as we have already seen, is the wisdom that makes one consciousness vibrate in perfect sympathy with another. It is love, that longs for ever greater union ; though utter unity, like utter freedom, is only possible in ânanda. Understanding and comprehension are both words which imply an activity of mental power or thought, and the great hunger of the man who has kriyâ as his predominant principle is to grasp the scheme of things entire. In the chapter on the fourth ray I will explain the appeals to man of the principle of harmony. All that need be mentioned here is that people of this ray are balanced between the seeking within and the advancing without, and are happy only when they can harmonise the claims of both the inner and the outer in their lives.

Now, races and nations, like men, have their dominant principles, and I can best illustrate the remainder of the scale by saying that in the early days of Aryan history, and even to-day in India, it is the first three ideals that have the strongest appeal; we find men seeking God within, as they would express it, along these three lines, which are to be seen with special clearness in the great schools of yoga of Patanjali, Shrî Krishna and Shrî Shankarâchârya respectively. But when, in the evolution of the Aryan race we come to the middle point, to the Greeks, we find the principle of harmony making a great appeal, and the sages beginning to turn the race over, as it were, to an appreciation of God as sat, and the awakening of a great soul hunger among men for the discovery of God in the outer world as truth, goodness and beauty.

These three modes of seeking without correspond to those of inward seeking, for there is a correspondence between God without and God within, between God in nature and God in consciousness. This appears between ichchhâ and tamas, and therefore between the will in consciousness and the stability in things. Will is the stability of consciousness and materiality is, as it were, the wilfulness of things, stubbornness, tamas. Now, as will be explained more fully later, that is beauty, the eternal poise and balance of perfect material things, at rest or in motion.

As tamas corresponds to ichchhâ, so does rajas to jnâna. The latter in man is love, the energy of consciousness that brings and holds together the many living beings; the former appears in him as desire, gathering together all things, and seeking the universal bounty. The ideal of God as goodness makes men seek Him in or behind nature as the bountiful giver ; God is worshipped as the sum of all good things.

The correspondence between kriyâ and sattva is that between thought and the laws of nature, which constitute the truth about things. The man who seeks the truth by the investigation of the world is the one who feels that there is a truth or reality in it which is the last of all things, before which all must bow. It is the predominance of the last three ideals in the later Aryan races that has brought to the front in their lives the three great forms of worship of God in sat, or nature, which are commonly called science, devotion and art. If there is any obscurity about the second of these, let it be remembered that the European nations in their places of worship are bowing to God and reverencing Him as the owner and dispenser of good things, and are appreciating Him principally for what they call His goodness.

The correspondences between the inward and outward seeking paths, the ideals that govern them, and their expressions in human affairs, are shown in the following diagram:

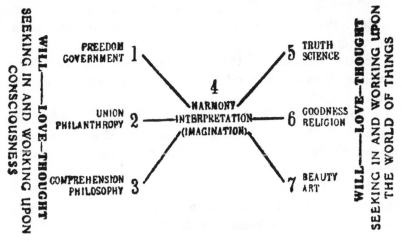

CHAPTER X

INTER-RELATIONS

I HAVE explained that Shiva is one, and that His unity is not disturbed by the presence of Vishnu and Brahmâ, who exist in Him and are each triple. Shiva is also essentially seven, as the foregoing statement indicates, and as I have said before. The principle which He keeps is sometimes called the synthesis of the other six, but is really the one principle, not made by the joining of the others, but being that from which they are derived by deduction.

Vishnu and Brahmâ exist side by side throughout the age of manifestation or day of Brahmâ, and are kept in harmony by Shiva through His yoga-mâyâ. The inter-relations between the three are then illustrated in the diagram on the following page.

Shiva touches all the six principles, as separate from the one, through His mâyâ, but Himself remains the one ânanda.

Vishnu turns towards Shiva through ichchhâ, and contacts Brahmâ through kriyâ, and in Himself remains essentially jnâna, love, the universal consciousness or heart.

Brahmâ turns towards Vishnu through rajas, and Shiva through tamas, and remains in Himself essentially sattva, law, or the universal mind or world of ideas.

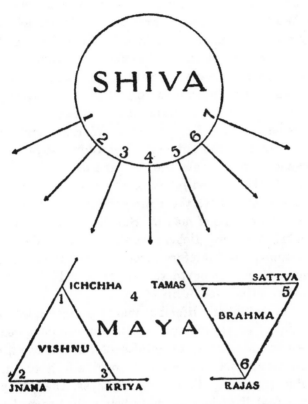

Every man's consciousness is a portion of Vishnu or chit, and all the evolution through all the planes spoken of by Theosophists is the expansion of his consciousness to include more and more of Vishnu, who is the Theosophical Logos, and has been called by some the God or supreme consciousness of this system of worlds. He is not the Universal God, but the God of consciousness, and His triple nature is ichchâ, jnâna and kriyâ. To understand this do not think of planes at all, but try to realise that Vishnu is the entire and all-embracing consciousness of the system.

The great triangle in the Occult Hierarchy of our globe is an important part of Vishnu, of whom every man's consciousness is a smaller part. Its three members—the Lord of the World, the Buddha, and the Mahâchohan—therefore represent the ichchhâ, jnâna and kriyâ of the solar Vishnu. They do not represent Shiva, Vishnu and Brahmâ. But since Vishnu keeps in touch with Shiva and Brahmâ all along the line of consciousness, not merely at the solar Headquarters, these great officials perform that office for the world-consciousness. The Lord of the World therefore looks, as it were, towards the universal God, Shiva, so that our globe consciousness may know the self and do its will; the Lord Buddha holds the united jnâna of our globe and presents it to the solar Vishnu. Both these are somewhat hidden functions —beyond the realms of mâyâ. But the Mahâchohan, directing the kriyâ of our globe, uses that power to deal with the triple Brahmâ, and therefore through mâyâ to relate the consciousness of our globe to the triple world of matter. He has thus five principles in his charge.

All life is Shiva's life, but men are passing through the Vishnu phase of experience, so, though each one belongs to one of the fundamental principles of Shiva's one life, he is now showing his essential nature through a form of consciousness. But remember that consciousness, the time process, is not his real life; just as mere being, the space process, is not his consciousness. Just as he uses a portion of Brahmâ for his body, so he uses a portion of Vishnu for his consciousness, but his real life is beyond consciousness.

Now, as Shiva, his true God, is equally one with Vishnu and Brahmâ, he can, while in the conscious state of mâyâvic life, seek Him by turning his consciousness within *or* without, to the universal principles expressed through Vishnu *or* Brahmâ. Will, love and thought thus become dual, inward turning to consciousness or outward turning to matter, according to the ray of the person enjoying that consciousness.

Still, although each man is living within the trinity of
consciousness, as he comes from Shiva he is himself septenary,
and all the seven principles are inseparable and present in
every man, but the one that is strongest in his nature is
called his ray. The ray of a man is therefore not only not a
material thing, but also not even a distinction in consciousness, but belongs to him in his relation to Shiva. It can
therefore never be *seen*, because sight is one of the senses,
however high its plane, and its object is always the gunas,
sattva, rajas and tamas. Consciousness is never *visible*, much
less *real life*, ânanda. Yet if a man is visibly working on a
certain line and has appropriated types of matter (life in the
phase of sat), for his vehicles and purposes, it may be inferred
that his ray has probably directed his choice of work and
determined the characteristics of his body.

When we speak of a man's ray, and thus think of his
predominant principle, let us not forget this fact that he has
all the other principles as well, and also that we are speaking
of a *man*, that is to say, of one who is the master of
himself to such an extent at least that his life is guided
from within his consciousness, and is not a mere set of reflex
actions or obedient responses to environment. A man who
is seeking God through his ideal is positive, not submerged in
sat and overcome by it, as are undeveloped men. He is
using his powers of thought to discover truth, or of feeling to
discover the goodness of things, or of will in work to find and
reveal beauty. All these activities are quite different from
the servitude and negativity of the embryo of man who lives
to no purpose but to indulge in idle, careless and selfish
pleasure.

The rays of animals are clearly marked, but not so those
of men until they have made considerable advance in the
human kingdom, the reason being that in a very real and
natural sense there has been a fall of man. With the

development of his mental powers he has made for himself such a mixture of karma and laid himself open to so many influences, that usually the deep spiritual desires of the man himself are overlaid and obscured even from his own vision. Still, if anyone had the skill and patience to analyse this ordinary man, he would find that one of his principles was stronger than the others, and was leading the forces of his soul towards the universal aspect of himself.

In a man of character, who is not a servant to his body or the personal emotions connected with that body, or the fixed ideas that it has acquired, but has really some active will or love or thought in himself, with which he is guiding his life, the ray can be distinguished with comparative ease, and there are certain questions that he may put to himself which will help him to discover his own ray; but these I must reserve until the specific rays have been described.

In the common life of men, the rays are exhibited in the following general types :

1. The man of will, seeking freedom through mastery of self and environment; the ruler.

2. The man of love, seeking unity through sympathy; the philanthropist.

3. The man of thought, seeking comprehension through the study of life; the philosopher.

4. The man of imagination, seeking harmony in a three-fold way; the magician, actor and symbolical artist or poet.

5. The man of thought, seeking truth in the world; the scientist.

6. The man of love, seeking God as goodness in the world; the devotee.

7. The man of will, seeking the beauty that is God in the world; the artist and craftsman.

The expressions and activities of these general types are very varied; it will be seen in their more particular description in Part II that they respectively include the characteristics that have been ascribed to the rays in different lists that have been issued to the world.

Before closing Part I of this book, I should like to explain why I have used imagery and terms of Sanskrit literature instead of others more familiar to English speaking people. First, because I have myself learned these truths in those terms. Secondly, because (as in modern science and technology) it is desirable to have new words for new ideas, and the Sanskrit words are most suitable. These truths are world-wide and the language we use for them does not matter—so Christians, for example, may in their own reading of them substitute "The Father, the Son and the Holy Ghost" for Shiva, Vishnu, and Brahmâ, if they wish.

PART II

THE SEVEN RAYS

There are seven chief Groups of . . . Dhyan Chohans,
which groups will be found and recognised in every religion,
for they are the primeval Seven Rays. Humanity, Occult-
ism teaches us, is divided into seven distinct Groups.

THE SECRET DOCTRINE

CHAPTER XI

THE FIRST RAY

"SELF-RULE or self-dependence," said the Manu of our race, "is happiness; rule by others is misery." This sentiment suits the man of the first ray, because it is the first of the three rays of independence and intuition.

Men of these three rays are described as independent, because they do not look upon the world as teacher, as bounteous mother, or as beautiful home, so much as a land of adventure for the valiant will, the sunny heart or the aspiring mind, to which one has come as from a far country for deeds of prowess. Such a man is full of initiative because he does not wait upon things and events for his impulses to action, but is inclined to treat them all (sometimes without due respect) as pieces in a game that he is playing, materials for a plan that he is putting into execution. He is called the man of intuition because he deliberately uses his own faculties of thought and feeling in his game of life, and they grow by that exercise. He is desiring in the will more sensation of self, in the heart more sensation of life, in the mind more sensation of things—he is seeking God or happiness in those things of the inner consciousness and is using life for that, while others wait upon the great world without, with their power and skill of thought or will or feeling, and learn through the tuition that nature gives.

Both these great paths lead to the same result—an enlargement of the complete inner and outer life. For while a man is seeking the divine in nature, her beauty and bounty and truth are operating upon him and developing his soul powers ; and when he is trying to give full play to the powers that he feels in himself he finds that that can only be done by using them for the improvement of the outer world. Each man, therefore, is in reality retreating within and advancing without at the same time.

In the man of will on the first ray self-government is the dominant note. If you belong to this ray your sense of self will be strong (and if you are not well evolved in other respects it may be disagreeable as well) and will tend to give you a firmness amid things and events that scarcely anything in the world can shake or change, an inclination to be positive in action, and the courage to face life as an adventure and not take refuge or rest amid things. If you are very strong in this, there will be no "home" for you in all the wide world, but the dignity of the self will be the centre and balancing point of your being. This is not an outward dignity that insists upon recognition from others, or works for that—such working is a sign of dependence upon externals—but a high sense of the true state of man, of one's own being, and a shuddering horror of the foreign finger of obtrusive events or persons that may touch the holy shrine. As no one can see beauty without admiring it (though some may look at it without seeing), and as no one can see truth without reverencing it ; so no one who feels the touch of the self within can ever be anything but a jealous priest at its holy shrine. This dignity is far removed from pride ; such a man is too proud to be proud. It is not a feeling of superiority that makes it ; it involves absolutely no comparison with others, and no measuring of strength. You are willing to be one with others on equal terms and say

namaskâr to God or beggar. You are not interested so much
in what you are as in that you are. You are the man above
all without wishes, living from within.

In consequence of this living power that is felt in one's
life the great ideal of this ray is independence or life from
within, freedom from the constraints of environment and a
tendency to govern circumstances and find a way to make
them conform to your plans. On the chess board of life a
man of this type will always have a plan of attack of his
own in full progress at the earliest possible moment, and he
will ignore his opponent's moves as much as he dares, using
every move and piece available for the attack that he has
planned. It is characteristic of the will to seek its ends by
every possible means, or in other words to keep the mind
constantly to the task, so that sooner or later it certainly
finds the way to its goal.

It is this man's sense of his own divinity that sometimes
makes him say " I will " even when he does not know how he
can, for he has an unfailing intuition of the fact that the self
within is the final and absolute arbiter of its own destiny,
as it is the foundation of its own strength. In him
thought understands the self, devotion bows to it, the
hands work for it, and every other part of him loves
the self, and therefore he can really will with the whole
of his life and being. On account of this inner stability, this man is usually at his best in adversity, and he
views with friendliness the destruction that is always going
on in the realm of nature. Some people are terrified at
nature's grim law, and battle against it, but he sees it to be
only his own power on a larger scale, and loves it as the
strong man always does a worthy adversary. He appreciates
the value of work to the worker, and when something is well
done he feels the will behind it, and it stands to him as a
mood of triumph with which he can ride upon the forces of

9

the world—just as in a smaller way an experienced swimmer knows that he is safe in the water, and semi-consciously puts on the mood before he enters into it ; and just as it is the swimming that is good, not the water, so this man is under no delusion as to the intrinsic value of external things. He does not work to attain the satisfaction of gaining some material position for the sake of rest or comfort afterwards, so destruction and failure do not depress him. When some new purpose is in hand, he is always ready to clear the decks for action, and let the old things go, or push them out of the way, and perhaps he is sometimes a little impatient of unnecessary things, and of persons who intrude into the work unnecessary feelings and thoughts and words.

He generally has a plan afoot, and, when that is finished, another in its wake, as regular as the waves of the sea. You sometimes come upon him in his mood of destruction, tearing up with great glee old letters and papers, casting old books out of his library, throwing away old furniture and clothes, or in the course of travel shaking himself free from them as a dog shakes off water. He is preparing to step forth upon some new adventure, in the pride of his naked strength, limbs free and nostrils aquiver. That spirit of destruction is not seen in the man of the second ray, who cherishes each thing because it speaks of human care and labor, and embodies something of the soul and energy of man. I knew a highly spiritual man of that ray who would always cut open the old envelopes which came to him, and use the blank insides for his own writing, not because he was parsimonious, but because he loved the works of man, though to himself he called his action economy and dislike of waste. The third ray man will look twice, and thrice, and yet again, at the object that is no longer needed, and then store it away, saying that perhaps some day it will come in for something else.

The man of will has not yet had his day in the department of political economy, but when that comes it will be seen that he respects the consumer as much as the producer; to put it crudely, he might say that people ought to be paid for eating food and using up other articles, just as much as for making those things; except that, of course, when his day of ideal anarchy does come, in some remote future, after mankind has learned the lesson of brotherhood, no payment to anybody will be necessary at all.

The self is sacred. No wonder, therefore, that people respect their personalities, when that is all the self they know, and that personal indignity and ridicule is the greatest torment to men who have not yet very clearly felt the self within. It is not good policy in life to despise the personality, for the god behind the idol is a real one; and if it plays the devil or the fool for the time being, its strength in that comes from the god within, who will presently emerge in his true character. The personality is thus a man's true companion and best friend on earth, even if he seems sometimes to act like an enemy.

It is the same will in man that gives a sense of reality to things, and makes "my experience" the last test of what is real, so that all thinking and feeling rest upon it. The testimony of others is valueless if it conflicts with that, and if the man of this ray follows a teacher it is not that he has become subject to another, for the teacher is accepted more as a guide than an instructor; and when he follows a leader or captain it is because he chooses so to do. If the captain says: "You must," he will reply: "I will," and if the captain retorts: "You must because I say so," he replies: "I have decided to obey you, and in doing so I therefore obey myself." He may not be conscious of it in this clear way, but the fact is that for him there is no way but to follow the self within.

A person of this ray feels that life is for action, and the
need of decision in practical matters therefore presses upon
him strongly. If he suspends judgment in any matter it is
not because of indolence of the will, but because he decides
to suspend judgment, but he will comparatively rarely do
this, and will prefer to decide temporarily and subject to
future revision rather than not at all. He feels that he must
make his move in the game, even when he does not see clearly ahead. He may therefore find himself learning much
more from the experiences that come as a consequence of his
actions, than from thinking about what may happen if he
acts in a certain way. There is also some danger of fixity in
his decisions, so that he may not be as open as is desirable to
reconsider a question or action. He has decided, and will
not reconsider and redecide unless he deliberately decides so
to do, and the occasion for that is sometimes hard for those
who have to work with him to arrange ; and it may even be
that sometimes unknown to himself he will take it for grant-
ed that because something is in a decided state in his
own mind it must be so in fact, and will project his own
strong inner conviction into the realm of nature and think
that the thing is so, and be unwilling to go and see whether
it is so or not. All this is due to the simple fact that the will
is his strongest principle and is constantly on duty governing
his thoughts and emotions and polarising them to its prevail-
ing purpose or mood.

The ultimate moods of our being are deeply hidden in
the self, and the will is thus but the self turned to the succes-
sion of events. As the destiny of all men is one, they are all
willing the same thing at the core of their being, and only because of this fundamental unity is complete freedom attain-
able. In the meantime, if the yogî in meditation is called
rock-seated, we may say that this man stands like a pillar of
iron. His temporary freedom lies in his ability, like that of

some of the old Stoics, to refuse to pay attention to the things that lie quite outside his government, for he is perfect master of himself, and therefore of all that is in the world within his power. It would not matter to such a man if he were alone in an opinion, and all other men stood against him; no doubt about its truth would be reflected upon it on that account for him. If he were otherwise a well-developed man, he would of course give those other opinions the most respectful consideration, but that is all. Having set himself also a standard of conduct, this man can keep it in the midst of an unsympathetic world, standing alone, for he never takes his color from the outside; whence he is chosen by the Guardians of Humanity to initiate new modes of life on earth.

Since the will is the faculty of self-change, self-control and the practice of austerity are easy for the man in this path. The first ray man rules himself with a rod of iron. If such a man learns that flesh foods, for example, are bad to eat, from a physical or moral point of view, he will give them up without effort, and if the body raises its head and says: " Oh, I do want the taste of venison again, and do you mean to say that you will not let me have it even for the whole long future of my life?" his reply comes without hesitation: " Yes, I mean just that." If he thinks that certain exercises or practices are good, he will do them, and the reluctance or inertia of the body will not deter him. In all this there will be no tension nor excitement, for the simple reason that the will is the quietest thing in the world. Sometimes people think that the big, blustering dominant person is the man of will, but that is not so; such a man uses that method because he thinks it is an effectual way to make others obey him, and he thinks so because he semi-consciously knows that he himself can be moved by blustering things acting upon him from the outside—a thing to which the man of will will never submit. No, the will is the quietest thing in the world.

And the man of self-control will not think of his austerity as an end in itself, but merely as the good life of the pure self whose purity is sacred not as a possession or an achievement, but as his very being.

Among the Hindus we see in a large and national way perhaps the greatest measure of this power. There are many people in India who care little for outward things so long as the self is satisfied within, and sometimes in practical affairs you will meet with people who are strong in this, but deficient in some other parts of their nature, and will find them utterly willing that you should think that you are having your own way and should be happy in that illusion, while inside they are enjoying a realisation that they are having their own way. The first ray is often a strangely silent path, and even the sound that is heard within is a voice of the silence, and on its path of yoga that silent sound is the man's guide far more than any visual clairvoyance. Amid the practical philosophies, that of Patanjali in India is typical of the ray ; his Yoga Sutras contain the teaching for the man of will. He proposes kaivalya or independence as the goal of the pupil's striving, and self-control of body, senses and mind as the steps to its attainment. Even in its preliminary course, while it speaks of the necessity of reverencing the divine in all things and thus attaining right knowledge, this school places first the work of tapas, which rightly and broadly understood means self-control and self-mastery in every respect.

Among the Greeks and Romans this ray gave birth to the Stoic school, and especially among the Romans this aspect of that great philosophy was brought to its highest fulfilment. Then every man who was really a Stoic felt the dignity of the self—a man could step out of his burning house and see his life's work in ruins, and say that he had lost nothing, since there were no riches outside the self. This was a thing that he felt for a fact, and knew to be so, since he would determine that the experience, painful though it might be, should be made to enrich his life.

I have not spoken of the faults of the ray, because there is no such thing of any ray. It may be that a man of one ray is not up to a general good standard in the other principles of his constitution, and in such a case the man of will might prove rather self-centred, overbearing, cunning, reckless, rude, inconsiderate, incautious or what not in the pursuit of his purposes; yet those faults are not to be ascribed to his strength in one line, but to his deficiencies in the others, and the way to remedy them is not to destroy the power that he has, nor to discourage the urgings of his essential character, but to direct these into better channels, so that he may realise how much richer his life may be and how much grander its scope when he learns to love and to think as he has learned to will, when he learns to respect all that is beautiful and gracious and good in the wonderful world of being that is God's school for all of us.

Sometimes in children you find this will in a curious stubbornness. The child wants to do something and is in fact about to do it, when some indiscreet elder happens to tell him that he must do that thing. Then the delight is all poisoned, and the child in loud objection or in silent stubbornness resists. I heard of a little boy, some six years old, whose mother wanted him to wear a certain shirt, but she had put it before him in a way not agreeable to his temperament, so he indignantly refused. The father was called in. The boy had no real aversion to the shirt, and was eager for a few words of kindness which would enable him to yield, but the father struck him, and then between his teeth he said: "Now I will not wear it, even if you kill me!" Ignorant parents and elders try to break the spirit of such children, to make them more graceful and obedient, and sometimes they do succeed in converting them into commonplace and respectable good people, whose goodness is for the most part good for nothing, either for themselves or anybody else. Such goodness is just not badness, as most people's idea of peace is just not war. Had the child been treated with love it would have responded, and to its will love would have been added, and in the later life of the grown man there would have been love with power behind it, with which great things might have been done in the world.

Should the work in the life of a man of the first ray involve him in the government of public affairs, and that is a duty that often falls to his lot, he will do it well, because in self-government he has found his own power of freedom. If, then, he be also a man who loves his fellows, he will be striving to bring that freedom to others, not by imposing regulations upon them from the outside, but by coaxing the will in them into greater prominence in their lives. The pure and good man of every ray desires only to give to others the joy of the ideal that he has found for himself, and if he be wise as well, to use his power also in service of their ideals.

CHAPTER XII

THE SECOND RAY

THE characteristic of the second ray is love, the positive expression in life of that wisdom which perceives through sympathy the state of consciousness in other beings, and takes it into account in dealing with them. It is also a ray of initiative, because love is the active energy of the soul, the rajas of consciousness, and all its activities tend to promote brotherhood and make our unity with one another more complete in life.

Persons not of this ray, though capable of feeling much sympathy for others, in their pleasures as well as their pains, though realising the benefits that accrue to men through their co-operation, cannot so easily realise that the union is not an arrangement but a fact, that brotherhood is more than co-operation, because it implies feeling, where co-operation does not. When this sense of union is sufficiently established in any man's heart, he will find himself not thinking of others from his own standpoint and considering how his own life is enriched and his own purposes forwarded by them, but in touch through some subtle feeling with their consciousness, so that he is as much interested in their lives and their purposes as in his own. The sphere of this sensitiveness goes on enlarging as the man of the second ray evolves, and he becomes the ideal father or mother, the ideal citizen, the

10

ideal patriot, the brother at last of all humanity, so that
whomsoever his eye lights upon, that person he loves.

He holds thus within his heart the solvent of all social
ills, the great power of love, and not the least of his virtues is
the universality of that love, which makes him respect not
only those who are similar to himself, and flattering to him
in that similarity, but also those who are quite different in
degree or in kind ; nay, more, it makes him almost revere
those who are different from himself, as possessing some part
of the great and all-lovable light of consciousness which he
has not been able to include in the small portion of it that is
his own. For his happiness, it is not necessary that he should
possess the means of entertainment and enjoyment, but it is
imperative that others should have them, and so all his
activity flows out in altruism, and perfect love has cast out
both fear and greed, and most of the causes of possible human
conflict I heard of a poor man who sat near a rich man's
gate, and was able to enjoy the rich man's pleasures without
the burden of his possessions ; as he watched the happy and
prosperous people passing, and looked at times into the win-
dows of the great emporia he had all that he could want.
I heard, too, of a man who, returned from a journey, found
that he had lost his valuable gold watch, and did not mourn :
" Alas, alas, I have lost my watch," but with a little glow of
delight exclaimed : " Why, someone must have found that
watch ! " These are perhaps ideal specimens of men of the
second ray, but they clearly indicate the type.

True men of the second ray are willing to suffer for their
love, yet no doubt the ecstasy of it hides from their eyes the
sacrificial nature of much of their lives. They are not the
people who help others who are suffering merely in order to
remove their own suffering which they feel through sympathy, whose first care is to avoid scenes of suffering and remove them if possible far beyond their sight so that they may

be forgotten. They are ready to face the world with all its imperfections, and its mixture of pleasures and pains, and humbly say: "Only God is good, and all this is just better and worse; but room for rejoicing at all times there is because the worse is always becoming better, and because every act of kindness, of comradeship or service, serves the betterment which at last will lead to all that we can think of as good." The doctrine of the evolution of life upward and onward for ever appeals to people of this kind and fills them with an energy that makes their love no mere sentiment, but causes it to overflow in service to the utmost of its capacity.

There is a reason why the evolutionary hypothesis should appeal strongly to people of this ray; it is the law of love expressed in life in the world. Take its most effective definition, as given by Herbert Spencer many years ago. He said it involved a progressive change from a state of incoherent homogeneity to one of coherent heterogeneity of structure and function. That means in simple terms that each organism in the world bearing and expressing consciousness is becoming a more definite and independent thing, with ever more decided character of its own, but at the same time is being drawn into a unity with others, in which its own function is employed for the advancement of more than its separate self. It means also that things which before were similar and separate are becoming different but united, and in the ideal end law and order will have triumphed over chaos and the dark, and all the channels will have been perfected for the universal interplay of life on earth as it is in heaven. To be a part of that advancing tide of consciousness is the delight of the second ray man, and he will not repine because the tide is not higher, but will take all the lives around him for what they are without foolish and complaining criticism, and will use all the power of his being to help them to unfold a little more. This path of human development has been called in

India the karma yoga. I know that statement is revolutionary, but it is correct, and the popular idea is wrong that takes the word karma, work or action, as the essential in describing this path, and overlooks that love of man which makes karma into karma yoga. Shrî Krishna taught the path of love, divided into two great branches, one of which was the bhakti yoga, devotion to God, and the other the karma yoga, devotion to man. What could be clearer than his instruction to Arjuna? "Verily as Janaka and others reached perfection by acting with a view to the unity of all people, so ought thou to do."

It is impossible, therefore, for the true second ray man to shrink from the world of action and say: "It is not good enough for me," or to despise the claims to his service that arise in large and small ways on every hand. It is his nature to go about doing good. With him it is not: "This is good to do, and that is bad to do," in rigid form; but to make anything better than it was before is good to do. I know a certain judge who stands at the head of a High Court of Justice in a country where the law still requires that murderers shall hang. The sole thought of that judge's life as a private man and a true Hindu is to do all the good that he can and to injure none, yet all the same now and then his duty requires that he shall sentence a murderer to death. Some time ago some of his spiritual friends approached him, and said: "Is it not inconsistent with your ideals to be responsible for the death of your fellow-creatures, even though they be inferior men? Ought you not to resign the post that requires this cruelty of you? Why do you consent to be the agent of so wicked a law?" The judge pondered the matter deeply, and at last came to a clear decision that he must not leave his post, for, he said: "Where I, loving even the murderers, send one man to his death, because I cannot save him, it may be that my successor, not loving as I do,

will send four men to their death; and if it be that karma
strikes me for the man that I have doomed, I must bear it for
the sake of the three men whom I have saved." That man
was not violating the law of love, was not taking the life of
one that another might be saved, but was fulfilling that law
to the uttermost and saving lives.

I knew also a lady who lived in a crowded town where
arrangements were very primitive for the disposal of stray
cats and dogs. Two men were employed by the municipality;
one to bring in the stray animals, the other to put them to
death, and each of these men was paid according to the
number of animals with which he dealt, which had the brief
respite of but three days between their capture and their
death. This lady, who loved animals dearly, and could not
bear to think of their danger and suffering, joined with some
friends, and they formed a society, with some well-known
and responsible people in the offices of dignity. They then
approached the municipal council and offered to take from
their hands all their trouble about stray animals. The
municipality assented, and gave them the use of an old
building and yard, and the lady became manager of the
institution. They employed a man on a fair regular wage to
go round with a Ford van and bring in the cats and dogs.
They kept the animals kindly for three weeks, and notified
the entire town as to where missing pets could be found, or
new ones obtained, and only at the end of that time did they
put the unwanted ones to death; and such was the humanity
of that lady that this worst of all offices she performed with
her own hands, that it might be done as humanely as could
possibly be. The second ray person is not doing good for the
selfish enjoyment of it, but because of love in the heart.

This is the ray of brotherhood. The second ray man
goes about doing good. He feels that good-will, friendship
and affection are the cement in the building of the temple of

humanity. He sees that schemes, regulations, agreements and co-operation will not go far in that work—that without love they cannot purchase peace for mankind.

People of this ray make the best teachers and doctors. I remember to have read some twenty years ago an article by the celebrated Oxford Professor, Bernard Bosanquet, in which he said that it was not advisable to employ the most brilliant scholars as teachers in schools, because these men had learned their subjects with the greatest ease, and were not in a position to understand the state of mind of the average student ; and certainly the quality of love is needed more than anything else, not only in education, the unfolding of the human powers in a child, but even in instruction, the imparting of knowledge. And everybody knows how, in most cases, the doctor who is able to take a real living interest in the patient is not only most popular but also most successful.

There are many departments of life open to people of each ray, at all levels of evolution. In the political economy of our time, as apart from what are called the professions, the second ray man should be the ideal distributor, whether as wholesaler or as shopkeeper. He will feel himself there to bring to the people just what they need, to be a real convenience and to circulate to them the kinds of things that will be serviceable to them. He will make himself a judge of the honest merits of the things he sells ; his prices will be marked with a fair proportion of profit, and he will avoid the things that have been produced by inhuman means. It is the fashion to regard business as a mere means of obtaining money, and to think that good can be done only outside it, but the simple fact is that here is one of the grandest opportunities for service to mankind.

It is sometimes thought that easy friendship is a sign of this ray, but that is not the case. I once knew a gentleman who was an exceedingly quiet man, and in a long life had made no friends beyond his immediate family. I asked him one day how this came about, and he said: "The fact is, I cannot play at friendship; if I make friends I must stand by them in every way, in all their troubles and difficulties; and as I have only enough for my wife and children, and must not risk what they need, I will make no friends." Here was a man of very great heart combined with third ray thought, ever ready to sacrifice his own pleasures or amusement for the sake of others, but in a perfectly unobtrusive way.

There are, of course, no faults on any ray, but people of the second ray can show very serious faults if they happen to be below a reasonable standard in the qualities of the other principles. There are many persons in the world who suffer very much when they think of some of the horrors which lie beneath and sometimes on the surface of civilisation. They are doing nothing to remove them, because there is little of will or practicality in their natures; but they go about making themselves miserable and disturbing others with the perpetual complaint that nearly all the power and money in the world have somehow got into the hands of people who do not love their fellow-creatures. If they were busy using all the small energy they already have in what little good they were able to do, they would not be adding their own disagreeableness to the existing sum of human misery, but would be preparing themselves for the exercise of greater power in the future. It is a condition in this world of law that no man shall have any power or opportunity for which he has not worked.

Similar to this also is the fault of carrying altruism to lengths that are absurd, as when the poet Goldsmith threw all his bedding through the window to some poor wretch wandering in the street below in the middle of the night. It gives no happiness to others to know that you are suffering on their account, and people who do not do what they ought to do for themselves, to make their own lives presentable and a cheerful part of the environment of others, are a serious misery to the world. Outbursts of what may be called generous anger are also not uncommon on this ray ; while the first ray man is more apt to retreat into the icy distance when the occasion is upsetting to him, and the third ray man is more liable to fear.

There is also a very frequent danger that great love without liberality of nature in other respects may be injurious rather than beneficial to the one who is loved, when it exerts a cramping effect. A story has been told about a young lady in America who lived with her mother and a younger sister in a little flat, and supported them by her earnings in an office in the town. In due course the young lady fell in love with a young man, who wanted to marry her and take her away from her office duties and set up a home, but, much to the distress of both of them, she could not do it because there was her mother to consider, who was always not quite well and there was also a younger sister, whose notions of her own future required that she should go to a rather expensive school, although she was far on in her teens. While they were in this impasse, her employer, an elderly gentleman of a benevolent turn of mind, and a shrewd observer, got to know about it, and very soon saw that the mother and younger sister were not really profiting in either body or character by the self-indulgent habits into which the kindness of his employee had gradually led them. He therefore took the rather startling step of calling her into his office one day and sternly dismissing her on the spot. There was no prospect of another situation for her just then, and things began to look black in the family fortunes, for the people had been living up to their income. But the remedy soon proved effective, for the mother realised that she must do something herself, and went to work in a store, where she soon forgot to remember her little ailments, which departed incontinently under such cool treatment, and she made many friends, so that her life became bright and strong; while the younger sister put aside some of her high-flown dreams and went to earn part of her schooling during the holidays. The two young people got married, and lived happily ever afterwards in the benignant shade of the former enployer's fatherly friendship. It is all right to lift a lame dog over a stile, but it may be foolish and unkind to carry it all along the road.

CHAPTER XIII

THE THIRD RAY

NOT long ago I came across an advertisement bearing a picture of a young man standing, with a girl beside him, buying chocolates at the counter of a sweetmeat store. It bore the legend: "Johnston's chocolates: From the Man who Understands, to the Girl who Knows." The girl knew what chocolates were good—that was fifth ray knowledge; the man understood what those chocolates meant to the girl—that was third ray comprehension.

The man of the third ray is sensitive to things as the man of will is sensitive to self and the man of love is sensitive to the consciousness in other living beings; and yet, because he is within the first three rays, among those who seek the self or God or happiness within, he is interested in things only for their bearing on conscious states. He is the philosopher who wants understanding or comprehension and feels that happiness depends upon that, that though the world might pour its bounty lavishly upon men and all be at peace in brotherhood, yet happiness would be lacking were there no means of understanding the significance of all these things to the soul. He is active with regard to things, but only in the interests of consciousness.

Understanding is at last the state of the mind in which it grips the world at large in one great comprehensive thought, which satisfies the soul, and the aim of one whose ray this is is not first to get knowledge but to satisfy this hunger of the soul. If this power of his that can see many things together, and can therefore comprehend them, is turned outward to the business of life, we find that this is the man with a splendid head for organisation and engineering, who can see the way in which things ought to be done. When that power is combined with the will of the first ray it may give great genius along those lines. His special power is thought, and working with persons of the first and second rays, he can see just how things of all kinds ought to be arranged so that their love and purpose will be most effectively bestowed.

Ask a person of this kind what he will do about some practical matter, for example, the employment of a teacher in a school of which he may have charge, and he will reply: "Give me ten minutes to think about it," and probably he will begin to ask questions, not because he wants anyone to think for him, which he abhors, but because he wants information on which his thought may be soundly based. He is a cautious man, and if perchance he is seriously lacking in some of the other principles he will sometimes be found to think so carefully about the thing in hand that the opportunity to do it has gone by before he has quite decided what is best to do.

The power of this ray gives to people a very broad mind, and the opportunity to carve out a path in life along many different lines, but because of this freedom from compulsion, and the breadth of opportunity that the third ray man thus enjoys, it sometimes turns out that it is so difficult for him to narrow himself down that he fails to concentrate on one line with sufficient vigor to make what is usually called a success in life, where a person of narrower nature, concentrated by his own limitations, would go in and win.

He wields the power of thought that moulds matter, and may turn to science or art or magic or to any other thing, and is not limited by the predilections which give such intense power along particular lines to some of the other rays. When a man concentrates he uses the power of his will to bring his attention to a strong focus and keeps his thought within this limit ; when he meditates he makes himself one with the thing by giving its every part the fullest possible attention and admitting into it all his thought upon the subject, but when he contemplates a third act takes place, in which he as it were fixes his perfected thought—and then the thought-power in that mental image moulds or directs the material, governing the natural forces, as a magnet draws iron filings. It is the great creative power, employed by the solar Brahmâ in the beginning—not simply meditation, but something bigger than that, called sanyama' which begins with concentration and ends with contemplation, and opens the door to all accomplishments. The yogîs of all these rays will all practise the entire sanyama, but the concentration part of it will be the most perfectly done by the first ray man, the meditation part by the second and the contemplation part by the third. You can understand what power there must be in the Adept, in whom all these rays have been developed to human perfection.

In facing the problems of life the third ray man will always say : " The truth will make us free. Give us understanding—action is bound to follow, so we need not trouble about it. Let the truth be painful or pleasant, we want it. Never mind our feelings." If he fails in love or in action he does not feel stained, but a failure in truth will give him bitter remorse.

On account of his breadth of vision and his valuation of things only as food for the hungry mind, the third ray man sees all things as very much the same, but that same tends to be the best, not the worst. He is the sage spoken of in Eastern Scriptures, where it says that to such a man all things are very much alike, a friend or an enemy, gold or a lump of clay ; and this of course means not that gold is after all merely clay and not specially valuable, nor that friends after all are of no more value to the soul than enemies are usually considered to be, but that all things are valuable and significant to the man who opens his life to their use—clay is as precious as gold, an enemy is really a friend. Said Emerson: " To the poet, to the philosopher, to the saint, all things are friendly and sacred, all events profitable, all days holy, all men divine ; for the eye is fastened on the life, and slights the circumstance." The principle behind this was well expressed by Epictetus, when he said that God had sent him into the world for the sole purpose of perfecting his character in all kinds of virtue, and that there was nothing in all the world that he could not use in the fulfilment of that aim.

The third ray man sees that things which people commonly call adverse are so regarded only because they are disagreeable to the feelings or uncomfortably agitating to the mind filled with preconceived opinions, but that all of them can be turned to great profit when they are accepted in the right spirit as from the hand of God, who is the giver of all things. He sees also the significance of insignificant things, and the wonder of the commonplace. To him everything is wonderful, but nothing is mysterious. A blade of grass will speak to him of infinity, where others need a mountain or a universe of stars. When the scientist says: " There is no miracle," he will reply : " Nay, all is miracle." And yet both affirm the same thing—the unity of nature. He has always a reason and often several for everything that he does; and can discover the reason for things occurring outside himself. The ideal of this ray is Brahmâ himself, who could tell the Rishis or sages all about everything in the world.

The quality of viveka or discrimination enables the philosopher to distinguish the important from the unimportant with reference to any purpose in hand. A story is told in Japan that when the great Shogun, Ieyasu, died, and his body was buried on the Nikko hills, his successor in the Shogunate called upon all the Daimyos of the Empire to send each a lantern of bronze or stone to decorate the gardens round the mortuary temple. All did so, except one man who was too poor, but he volunteered instead to plant rows of trees along the road, for the shelter of travellers. His offering is now seen to be far more precious than all the rest —the third ray man would have seen that clearly from the beginning.

In his own person, this wonderful vision gives the third ray man singular adaptability ; he can live in hut or palace, and sleep upon the ground or a couch of down. And in his life he shows a great sensibility of the uses of particular things, a capacity to employ all kinds of materials that are available and build them into a plan. He is the chess-player *par excellence*, using all the pieces of different kinds according to their nature in a definite plan, nay, grasping many plans at once, so that he can see how if his move does not turn out well for one plan he may adapt it to another and make the most of every possible situation. And because in dealing with other people he has the same breadth of view, he cannot be fussy about small things, but knows what is important and what is unimportant, so that adaptability shows itself again in the form of tact.

The third ray man takes but little account of teachers, for everything is his teacher and he has the secret of contemplation, so that when he observes things the higher mental intuition flashes forth, from that region where pupil and teacher are one. " What have I to do with gurus," such a man once said, " who am a pupil of worms and fishes, frogs and trees and rocks ? " It has been observed that to find a specific teacher on this ray is more difficult than on the others ; it is as though the guru held off in order to make sure that his would-be disciple should learn his lessons from everything, as his ray demands. Emerson was typical of this ray, though also largely tinged with the first ray.

Sometimes it is possible to understand a great deal of human nature by the study of animals, and I have long thought that our brother the elephant, whom I have had the privilege of contacting to some extent in India, is very typical of this ray. You may watch him standing for hours in a busy market place, swaying gently from side to side, observing attentively everything that is going on, but showing not the least desire to take active part in it himself. It is said that when the elephant is first captured he is a demon incarnate, but is so much a philosopher at heart that the very moment when he understands that further resistance is useless. he accepts the new situation with perfect calm, and makes himself at home and agreeable under the new conditions. He is always very brave in facing any danger that he understands, but on the other hand is extremely timid in the face of comparatively slight things with which he is utterly unacquainted, so much does his life centre upon and rest in understanding. In a panic he loses his head, but under all other circumstances he is most considerate and careful, and in his affections, which are deep and lasting, solicitous to an extraordinary degree. In this the animal shows very clearly the ray, for the weakness of this ray is fear. If in the course of his evolution a man has relied upon knowledge to dispel his fears, he will continue to fear in some measure what he does not understand. For a similar reason people of love, of the second ray, are liable to bursts of indignation and anger, and those of will, the first ray, sometimes fall a prey to pride.

A man of this type will make most rapid progress by training his mind in both acute and comprehensive thinking. Especially, in order to make the most of this power, should he clearly image what he is going to do at any time. Have you ever seen an expert professional skater flashing about, his every movement as clean and inevitable as new steel? Or a penguin catching fish and full of unceasing and instantaneous and unerring motion? So may this man think, when he has trained himself—as the skater glides, as the penguin turns and goes. And to enlarge his mental grasp let him practise adding one thing to another in his thought—making each one perfectly clear to himself and then joining it to the growing idea. Thus he may think of a blade of grass and then of many, and add shrubs and flowers and trees to his picture, until soon he can hold a garden in mind without loss of detail, as before he held only a blade of grass.

CHAPTER XIV

THE FOURTH RAY

THE predominance of the fourth principle marks the man of the fourth ray. His quality is harmony. He cannot keep the internal worlds and the external worlds apart in his life. If he has an idea, it is unsatisfying until he has given it practical expression ; if he has work to do in the world, he is unhappy about it unless he can make it express an idea or an ideal. Among men he does not represent the inner alone (as do the governor, the philanthropist, and the philosopher), nor the outer alone (as do the scientist, the devotee and the artist). He exhibits the principle of mâyâ, which I have already described as a special expression of Shiva Himself, bringing Vishnu and Brahmâ together in harmony. No greater reality could there be on earth, and yet it is an illusion, because is it not the very life of Shiva Himself, the true ânanda. His activity is not of prakriti, (the material), nor of purusha, (the spiritual), not of sat (being), nor of chit, (consciousness), but it is what Shrî Krishna called "My other prakriti" (My other manifestation)—daivîprakriti— not merely mâyâ, but yogamâyâ. True above all it is in the experience of the man of this ray that there is no bar or wall in the soul where God ceases and man begins, as was said by Emerson.

In the earlier stages of his development the man of this ray will show strong moods, sometimes leaning towards the three types of self-reliance (the first three rays), and

12

sometimes towards the three types of devotion, (the last three rays), but he will never get quite away from his balanced position, from showing the simultaneous presence of both sides of human nature. This causes him much unhappiness; for in the work that he has to do in the world he feels the need of expressing an ideal; and ideals sear and burn his soul unless he can express them. He is thus the man of the uncomfortable conscience, until he reaches that blessed state of life in which his inner and outer parts have been brought into constant working harmony, and in which the great laws of outer and inner growth, karma and dharma, have blended into one. But when they *are* blended, there is for him the nearest thing to real happiness that is possible on earth; the interpretation of the inner to the outer and of the outer to the inner is full and constant, and sometimes the spirit of prophecy flashes out into expression.

The life and religion of Egypt exhibited very strongly the influence of this ray. The things of that land were representative of life, and the representations of life were very thingish in form. Take, for example, the architecture of the Egyptians, with its leaning lines and rounded and bellying pillars, and its constant subjection to animal and vegetable forms—not ornamentation with those forms. On the other hand, the sculpture and drawing of human figures and other living beings was in a more mathematical form than has been seen elsewhere. And all this was a fitting garb for the inner magic which was the very life of Egypt. It was art, full of a soul-stirring beauty—but symbolic art, whose beauty was open only to him who had the key. And as the Egyptians lived their symbolic stories they felt the reality behind them; just as when they felt the psychic truths they needed to express them in form.

Everybody may observe the influence of forms and colors on mind and moods. If you enter a room, for example, that is decorated with forms curved and flower-like, you will find that your emotional nature is stirred by them ; but if you enter one ornamented with squarish designs, you will receive a mental impression. That influence is direct, and there is much symbolism that operates in this way. But in addition, thought attaches to things and forms, and among thoughts like attracts like, so very many symbols have much thought-force connected with them. This can be felt by sensitive persons of the fourth ray. Many varieties of art magic have resulted from recognition of these truths. The practical magician on these lines belongs to the fourth ray.

We may see the influence of the ray in a great variety of human activities. The person who has it strongly developed will probably be very much of an actor. If he wants to produce a certain mood or state of mind within himself, he will do it by assuming its outer form ; for example, if he wants to feel pious or devotional he will assume the vestments and the manner of church or temple, and the conventional attitude of devotion of his country or religion, and then the inner state will spring up in response. People of this kind are to be found everywhere pretending to be what they want to become ; yet in this there is no real pretence, no hypocrisy, no desire to create an impression on others, but simply assumption that will very soon become reality. I heard of an English lady of this type who had been to India and had there become much enamored of Hindu philosophy and anxious that its teaching should permeate her soul. When she returned to London she insisted on dressing in the Indian way, and sitting on the floor to eat her meals. Her enemies laughed and her friends gnashed their teeth ; but she was obeying what was a right impulse for her.

People of the fourth ray also make good actors, because, when they produce in themselves the emotional states that they want to portray, the outward forms and actions that go with those states follow without special attention and with the greatest ease. The graceful side of physical culture and expression is theirs also (as seen, for example, among the Spaniards), because that is the expression of spiritual freedom in the body. Every variety of interpretation of mind to matter and of matter to mind is to be found among the multifarious activities of this ray. Magician, actor and symbolic artist or poet all have their place here.

In India, where everything is to be found to such an extraordinary extent that it seems to be a veritable epitome of the human race, the influence of this ray is seen strongly in art and in some forms of worship. If a Western person is fortunate enough (and it is a rare thing), through his own sympathy with them, to win the real friendship and confidence of a Hindu family, so that no part of their lives is hidden from him or modified in his presence, he may perhaps be permitted to see the things which occupy the shrine which exists in every Hindu home. There he will find images or pictures of the forms of the Deity, and sometimes of saintly men, which are far from beautiful according to the external canons of art. But he will soon discover that when his friend approaches these things he pays them the deepest reverence, and will exclaim with rapture about their beauty. The beauty is there, but in the mind of the beholder, and its living reality is awakened by the familiar suggestions of the pictures and images.

This is not entirely different from the use of language. The word "beauty" is far from beautiful itself, but as soon as it is spoken visions of the beauty that one has known rise before the mind. It is true that language can have beauty in addition to its meaning, but that aspect of it belongs to the seventh ray; the use of language for the expression of ideas is an art belonging pre-eminently to the fourth ray. The fourth ray man has usually great wealth of words.

We have seen that the first and seventh rays have will
dominant, that the second and sixth rays have love, and that
the third and fifth have thought. The fourth ray man, not
having come along any one of these lines, has usually all the
three powers of consciousness mingled more or less equally,
but none of them as perfect as he would have had it if he had
specialised on one of the other lines. The faculty that this
balanced condition gives to the mind is imagination, which
is a blending of will, love and thought. If a man of this type
starts to think out a problem, he is not likely to keep for long
to the logical sequence; his feelings will break in upon it,
and often the solution will leap into his mind, revealed by the
concentration of the will. If, on the other hand, his feelings
are roused by something, his logic will also come into operation, and show him perhaps the humor of the situation,
perhaps the purpose of the events.

In its positive form this imagination is a magical power,
and human life is full of it. Looking at things, its owner
sees the life; looking at life he sees the world of things. He
cannot give his attention to one alone. When power is
achieved on this line the man will be a real magician, linking
the seen and the unseen, producing visible results by invisible
means, and invisible results by visible means.

The literary people who are on this line show a great
wealth of imagery in representing their ideas, and their aston-
ishing power of analogy brings to their service images
from the uttermost ends of the earth. Great flights of fancy
such as those of Shakespeare and Kâlidâsa have their birth
in this faculty.

The power of imagination can be a very vivid thing, and
is often seen in singular power in the life of children. I heard
recently of two little girls who were talking about what they
would do when they were grown up, and one of them said
that she was going to have a nice home and a lot of children.

The other, who had evidently been brought up in a far from ideal environment, replied: " Yes, and I am going to have a school, and your children will come to it. And I shall smack 'em, and smack'em, and smack'em ! " she added with much gusto. The first little girl burst into tears, and between her sobs said: "Oh, you horrid thing, what have my children done to you that you should hit them like that ? " It is not very often that one finds imagination so vivid in later life, but probably it is more so in the great fourth or Atlantean race than in the fifth or Aryan. I knew a Chinese doctor who told me that the delight of his leisure hours was to lie back in his big chair and imagine that he was in heaven, and apparently the experience was so real to him that it was almost as good as the actual thing.

In Western lands the Irish people give us a good exhibition of the mental qualities of this ray. They often mix their faculties in a way that puzzles or amuses others, according as the occasion is serious or light. They bring in logic when it is least expected, and turn from reason to fancy in the same way. It is in fact a general characteristic of the ray, that its activities beginning in one line tend to end in another ; starting in mirth they will often end in melancholy ; starting seriously they may end in play. This is the origin of many Irish jokes. A story is told that one day a gentleman, taking a walk, came upon an Irish friend of his, who was digging by the roadside, and put to him the sort of futile question that people are apt to ask on such occasions. "Hallo, Mike ! " said he. "What are you doing ? Are you digging a hole ? " "No," came the unexpected reply, "I am digging the earth and leaving the hole." An inverted form of this occurred when a certain Irishman was to be engaged on a job of building work, and he was asked whether he was accustomed to climbing ladders, and replied, "No, sir, I have never gone up a ladder except once, when

I went down a well." The Teuton, who has made a fetish
of law, or rather rules, can rarely understand the simple
logic of the Irishman, who does not live by formula, and
will disregard regulations when it seems to him that they
are unnecessary.

I am tempted to illustrate this ray with a reference to
the animal kingdom, though I must mention it only with the
warning that in the illustration that I have chosen the ray is
exhibited in a very primitive form, into which human beings
only occasionally lapse. It is our cousins of the monkey
tribe who exhibit these qualities, as I have had the pleasant
fortune to see through occasional contact with them in their
native haunts. See them start out on some serious business,
and end up a moment later leaping and gambolling over one
another. See the pensive melancholy of their quietude, and
the utter playfulness of their activity, and the humor that
glances across between these states. How they laugh at
themselves, when they are not in the depths of despair or
thrilled with great enterprise. See the way in which they
pretend, and try to become by imitation, and see the
unfinished and variable character of all their works. I
cannot resist quoting a few lines, in conclusion, extracted
from *The Road-Song of the Bandar-log* of Kipling, who caught
their moods with true genius:

Here we go in a flung festoon,
Half way up to the jealous moon!
Don't you envy our pranceful bands?
Don't you wish you had extra hands?

Here we sit in a branchy row,
Thinking of beautiful things we know;
Dreaming of deeds that we mean to do,
All complete, in a minute or two—
Something noble and grand and good,
Won by merely wishing we could.

All the talk we ever have heard
Uttered by bat or beast or bird—
Hide or fin or scale or feather—
Jabber it quickly and all together!
Excellent! Wonderful! Once again!
Now we are talking just like men.

Then join our leaping lines that scumfish through the pines.
That rocket where, light and high, the wild-grape swings.
By the rubbish in our wake, and the noble noise we make,
Be sure, be sure, we're going to do some splendid things!

CHAPTER XV

THE FIFTH RAY

THIS and the following two rays show the general character of obedience, because through them the God within is seeking the God without. Strictly speaking, they are all rays of devotion. And the first of them that we have to mention is that on which especially the thinking part of man finds itself bowing in unquestioning service to the great mind of the world, the world of ideas, the universe of law, and puts itself under the tuition of that world. Truth is the name for the ultimate reality when it is seen in this way, and though the scientist in his constant search for more of it will examine and question everything else most unmercifully, he never questions the truth of truth or the fact of fact. He bows before them in completest and most delighted submission, because they are final reality, and when its face is seen its authority is evident to the soul.

To the fifth ray man the world's truth is the foundation of reality, and his search for knowledge is thus a great religious activity founded essentially on faith. Elsewhere I have formulated his creed as follows: "I believe in the world as a place where truth can be found; I believe in the human mind as an instrument for its discovery; and I believe that when it is discovered by man it will prove to be of benefit in his life."

13

If we contrast the state of the savage with that of the civilised man of to-day, the virtue of this creed will be seen. The savage has little peace of mind, for the simple reason that he does not know that he can think about everything. He accepts a great many things, like thunder and lightning, shadows and disease, as great mysteries, and when or where or how he will be struck by them he has little or no notion, but is full of fear of the event. But the civilised man knows a good deal about the world, and has enhanced the powers of his senses and the strength of his hands in a myriad ways too familiar to mention, from the benefits of which he does not escape even for one moment in all the day. Strange to say, with all this achievement at their constant service and ready as most men are to admire the triumphs that the science of the ages has won for us, they still regard some things as mysteries to which thought is not applicable, as, for example, the problem of death. The drawing of that line between what can and what cannot be known is a remnant of savagery, but the men of the great fifth ray, playing their part in human progress, will some day remove that prejudice and bring the knowledge of facts even about death within the mastery of man, long before even our Aryan race comes to an end. It is impossible to estimate the god-like heights of knowledge and power to which science will raise the life of humanity on earth in course of time. And that will come about because of the method of the scientist, who examines his facts with the greatest care, compares them with dispassion and without prejudice, hoping for no particular results, and accepts his thoughts about them as knowledge, his hypotheses as theories, only when he has tested them again and again.

To realise the faith behind science, recall for a moment those conditions in the middle ages of Europe when the light of knowledge was obscured by the cruel and cowardly men of the time who wielded paramount secular authority in the name of religion. They had decided that this was not really God's world, that He was somewhere else, and though He had put us here as souls upon probation, He was allowing our lifelong examination to be conducted by His great adversary the devil himself. So this world came to be thought of as the devil's world ; it was a place of untruth, and knowledge about it would lead men away to their damnation, and indeed the human mind, with which men proposed to make their mundane enquiries, was itself held to be so conceived in sin that never could it be an instrument for the discovery of truth of real benefit to man. Clearly men did not then know that the world was a place of truth, but there were a few who felt that it must be so, who had faith in it and themselves, and faith so strong that not all the terrors of the Inquisition could stop them entirely, and utterly put out the light of science. These few stood firm and gradually won their way to general acknowledgment, and proved the value of the fifth ray faith that was in them ; and to-day every intelligent religious devotee is ready to acknowledge not only that science has made physical life splendidly rich for man, and has raised it far above the animal lot, and enabled men calmly and peacefully to face all the problems of material existence, and develop the human mind by exercise to a splendid degree ; but in addition to all that it has assisted the devotee himself to realise God more perfectly.

At all times men have thought of God as the Master of the Universe, but when they considered that the world was nothing more than a somewhat large flat place, and that the sky was something supported on pillars, or perhaps a kind of inverted pudding-bowl, with little holes in it through which the light of the celestial regions might shine to form the stars, their conception of the grandeur and dignity of the Master of that Universe was not to be compared with that which rises for devotional adoration to-day ; when men think of the wonders of the large, of the millions of worlds in endless space, which have been revealed to us by astronomy ; of the wonders of the small opened up by chemistry and physics ; and of the marvels of the life in nature revealed by physiography and biology, which make the Universe inconceivably wonderful and open in it new vistas every day.

The devotional character of a fifth ray man is seen in the way in which he worships without question the laws of nature, and believes with ease in the immortality of essential matter. Never do you find him wishing to alter by a hair's breadth the working of the slightest of nature's laws, nor would he, were it in his power by the lifting of his little finger, dare to intrude a modification of his own into the adjustment of things ; so perfect seems to him the adaptation and organisation of this world, which is always his best teacher. He clearly sees that whenever anything is invented or made by man, nature through experience will cause him to improve upon it. He produces a motor-car, for example, but when he runs it on the road he will learn something new about it, which without external nature's assistance he could not have learned, and also in the process he will have developed a little further his power to know.

Were the scientist to philosophise a little, as is not very usual with him, we might hear him saying to himself that his smaller mind is perfectly adapted to the divine mind represented by the laws of nature, and is learning on that account, and further that it is growing ever richer and more powerful by exercise in an environment so perfectly suited to it. Were he also devotional and aspirational, he would add to this statement and say that the world acquaints us with the nature of God, as we have seen above, and also makes us more like Him. It brings us nearer to the omniscient in so much as it tutors the mind to a greater grasp of living reality in every moment of time, and brings to vision the truth that everything is infinitely significant to the wise man, though it may seem unimportant to the fool. With a little philosophy he would also realise that man does not wield power over the forces of nature by means of knowledge, but associates himself with those forces, and inasmuch as he works with them they work with him in a co-operation which reveals one of the greatest laws, that there is no real conflict in all the realms of nature, but all are working together for good.

Sometimes appreciation of law in nature impresses a man in such a way that he cannot escape from it even in the small things of life, and then he tends to make a fetish of plans, rules and regulations, when such things are unnecessary. I heard once of a man who numbered all his shirts and other articles of clothing and kept a card index of them, so that he could see at a glance where, say, number 9 shirt was—at the laundry, undergoing repairs, or in such and such a drawer!

I imagine that the animal of this ray is man's faithful servant, the horse, which before the plough or in the cart or under saddle, is learning to live a regulated life, and to respect rules and forms, law and order, and the inevitabilities of material life.

CHAPTER XVI

THE SIXTH RAY

JUST as the fifth ray shows skill in thought, go does this express skill in feeling; for they are feeling and thought directed to things. And just as the faith of the scientist leads him to penetrate to the principle of law in the world, so does the faith of the sixth ray man lead him to penetrate to the goodness that prevades or stands behind the world, and to surrender himself in all obedience and devotion to that, which is what most men mean by God.

All through the ages there have been devotional mystics whose prayers have contained no shadow of material request, but a flowing forth in perpetual thanksgiving and adoration at the feet of the great Goodness that drew them with compelling power and irradiated their lives with super-human joy. And these men and women realised by direct feeling what others might reach by argument, the fact that the experiences of life are not good and bad just because they are pleasurable and painful, but all are most profitable because all come direct from the hand of God. "Everything that is received is a gift," says a Hindu proverb, and verily so it seems to the sixth ray devotee. The true devotee must feel more goodness in things and experience than other men do, for he is more in touch with the heart of the world. At least he has caught a glimpse of the divine goodness in the world, and his devotion is a longing to realise more.

Though he does not usually know it, this path of his is a great means for the destruction of pain, which is so largely produced by the unruly imagination of man, which in early stages leads him to eat more than he can digest and grasp more than he can hold, and to long for incompatible things— a destruction so great that physical pain seems small beside the delight of his vision, and the honor of his service. He knows that what comes is good, even when he does not know how it is good, and one could formulate his creed as similar to that of the scientist and say : " I believe in the world as the place of God's goodness, and that the feelings of the heart, if encouraged, will lead to its ever greater discovery, and that when men trust in God and fear not their faith will be immeasurably rewarded even in the material world."

The simplicity of this faith is sometimes very touching, as readers of *The Little Flowers of Saint Francis* will recollect. I knew very well an Indian gentleman who was one of the foremost lawyers in his Province, who was strongly of this type. He was surprisingly trustful of fate, and would often go late for his train. What sympathy between him and events existed I do not know, but this is certain, that when he was late the train proved to be late too. Only once have I known him to miss the train, and then he said to me with his smile which was, I think, the sweetest that I have seen on earth : " Oh, well, what God does is best for us ! " This was his constant saying in all his troubles—which were numerous enough. Yet never was this man careless about helping others ; hundreds of people had cause for deepest gratitude to him, and when he died it was as though the whole town in which he had lived lost light.

It is the simplicity of devotion that is its spiritual strength. Not by spectacular gifts is God to be realised in His world, but by utter purity of worship. What says Vishnu, speaking through the *Gîtâ* ? " If a leaf or a flower

or a fruit or a drop of water is offered to Me with devotion, I
accept it from the aspiring soul, because it is presented with
devotion. *Whatever* you do, or eat, or sacrifice, or give,
or make an effort to achieve, do that as an offering unto
Me." No sweeter tale of this simple devotion has ever been
written than that of the village woman in *The Light of Asia,*
who thus spoke to the Lord Buddha:

" Worshipful ! my heart
Is little, and a little rain will fill
The lily's cup which hardly moists the field.
It is enough for me to feel life's sun
Shine in my Lord's grace and my baby's smile,
Making the loving summer of our home.
Pleasant my days pass filled with household cares
From sunrise when I wake to praise the gods,
And give forth grain, and trim the tulsi-plant,
And set my handmaids to their tasks, till noon.
When my Lord lays his head upon my lap
Lulled by soft songs and wavings of the fan ;
And so to supper-time at quiet eve,
When by his side I stand and serve the cakes.
Then the stars light their silver lamps for sleep,
After the temple and the talk with friends.

" For holy books teach when a man shall plant
Trees for the travellers' shade, and dig a well
For the folks' comfort, and beget a son,
It shall be good for such after their death ;
And what the books say that I humbly take.

" Also I think that good must come of good
And ill of evil—surely—unto all—
In every place and time—seeing sweet fruit
Groweth from wholesome roots and bitter things
From poison stocks ; yea, seeing, too, how spite
Breeds hate, and kindness friends, and patience peace
Even while we live ; and when 'tis willed we die
Shall there not be as good a ' Then ' as ' Now ' ?

                                    " But for me,
What good I see humbly I seek to do,
And live obedient to the law, in trust
That what will come, and must come, shall come well."

Then spake our Lord : " Thou teachest them who teach,
Wiser than wisdom in thy simple lore."

The Hindus and Buddhists say that the energy of the world is directed not without reference to the welfare of the beings that live in it, but solely for their good, and speak of the great law of karma, the moral law that pervades the universe, whereby no suffering can come to any living creature but what he has produced for himself by first inflicting it upon others. They say that therefore there is no cause for fear in this which is God's world. This law has ever been felt as a blessing without limit in the Buddhist religion, and reverenced as the greatest thing in all the world—the good law—and those who worship and found their happiness upon it may also in many cases belong to the sixth ray. In the many books that exist among the Hindus and Buddhists for the definite building of character, and improvement of man by self-culture, it is always taught to the aspirant that he must bow to God in everything, content, as it says in the *Gîtâ*, with whatsoever cometh to him through no immediate effort of his own, and willing to work with that as the best means towards the perfection of his life.

This longing for goodness in things can also attach sixth ray people with bonds of real gratitude to any great leader or teacher who proclaims the supreme goodness and shows the strength of its service in his own life. Such people have gathered, for example, to the standard of the Christ in the Western world, of Shrî Krishna in India, and of others of various degrees of eminence at all times. In Christianity you will find the three kinds of people who exist in every religion : the first, those who are under the sway of karma and show no definite ray at all, because they are not masters of themselves and their own lives, but live in fear and trembling and seek religion as a refuge ; and of the rest, those who reverence Christ for his love and service of man, and those who are ready to love and serve man in obedience to Christ, whom they reverence first because of His great goodness. Of these

14

latter the first group are people of the second ray moved by sympathy for the life around them, and the second group are people of the sixth ray, devotees first and servers afterwards.

An aspect of this ray that plays a big part in the reverence of the world, quite without personification, is the appreciation of prosperity. This world of ours is gratefully loved by millions of people who enjoy with zest the blessings of prosperity or of Lakshmî, and admire without stint Her presence in the big achievements and possessions of mankind. This is felt in greatest measure at present by the people of America, who love their cities and their fruitful plains with a devotion that knows no stint. "God's own country," they call it, with tears in their eyes, for they are a people not ashamed of feeling—and verily is Lakshmî there.

Among animals it is our friend the dog that best exemplifies this type. For him a master who can do no wrong, whose life is a round of miraculous powers, who is the source of all bounty, the being to be waited for, to be worked for, to be died for, who opens the gates of paradise in every walk abroad, whose very sternness is somehow kindness, before whom it is supreme and glowing dignity to grovel when he is displeased—this is the god of his salvation—and no truer devotee has Christ or Krishna among the ranks of men.

CHAPTER XVII

THE SEVENTH RAY

As the scientist sees the divine thought in nature, and the devotee worships the loving heart, so does the true artist respond to the skilled hand ; he worships the beauty of nature without reserve. This is the third of the rays of obedience or devotion, because the artist and lover of beauty acknowledges his Master in the great world.

The true artist does not regard himself as the creator of beauty, any more than the true philosopher considers himself to be the author of the truth that he proclaims. See the wisdom of the Platonist in this respect. He asks the question: "Where does the philosopher obtain his truth, and the artist his beauty ? Do these geniuses invent these things with the power of their own minds, and thus bring something new into the world ; or do they obtain them from the wonderful creation in which we live ? " And he answers the question to the effect that art is but a copy of nature, and the artist but a seer of the divine mind that fills the world with every kind of wonder, beauty among the rest.

I recall an occasion at the exhibition of the Bengal school of Art when some visitors stood before a fine series of paintings of sunsets in the Himâlayas and criticised them loudly, saying that surely such colors never existed in a sunset anywhere ; but later those same persons exclaimed on seeing a sunset again : " Why, there are the colors of those Calcutta pictures." They had not noticed them before, and they saw them now only because they had seen the paintings, and the artist had taught them to see in some measure what he saw himself.

The beauty in everything touches the artist, full as he is of physical sensitiveness as no one else, and it can lift him to heights of consciousness that others fail to realise as within its power. I remember a Russian artist who was convinced that there could be no hope for Europe until it responded to Russian art and allowed its influence to mould the civilisation and remodel the people. Realising this power, the Platonists added devotion to their philosophy, and saw that happiness must arise from the contemplation with profoundest reverence and gratitude of the works of the universal being in whom our life is lived. The ecstasy of beauty is to be a constituent of the perfect state of life beyond consciousness, ânanda itself.

Regarded in this light, the skilled artist becomes a co-worker with God for the evolution of man. Though he may be thrilled and irradiated with what flows to him through the channel of beauty, as all people are in the measure to which they can respond, this man has will to steady his thoughts and feelings, so that they flow through his hand in the form of work. That concentrates him in his devotion and helps him to neglect the opinions of the world. He first sees the beauty that others cannot see, and then reproduces it apart from the confusing mass of beauty with which it is mixed under ordinary conditions, and thus brings it to the attention of others.

Because the artist never loses sight of the God in things, he never tires in his aim, not through the whole of his life ; and the amount of sustained concentration, which is will, with which all his faculties are controlled in service of his work, is rare to behold. Think, for example, of the careful

and utterly devoted work put into every smallest bit of the
grand temples and mosques of India. Nearly all the towns
and large villages of South India are dominated by huge
temples with goparas covered with detailed carving and
moulding, and are beautified with tanks surrounded by
artistic walls, while in the centre and north of India there
are almost everywhere magnificent mosques with minarets
and domes, palaces and tombs, and temples of a smaller type
than those of the south. These magnificent erections,
beautiful in size, outline and proportion, as well as in
detailed features of carving, remain with us as enduring
monuments of former days, when men sought ecstasy and
revelation through beauty, and they are now a splendid
instrument for refining, elevating and enlarging the consciousness of all who live near them or visit them and are
moved by their surpassing beauty, and surely the rare grace
of the Indian people is largely due to the work of this ray in
their part of the world. Who the architects and sculptors
were we do not know, but looking upon their work we realise
with what patience and perseverance they must have labor-
ed year after year to make accurate and perfect every detail
of their work. Writers of many nationalities combine to
praise and thank those unknown artists for their labors,
which will continue for thousands of years to be an inspira-
tion to devotees of beauty throughout the world.

You cannot contemplate such beauty without yourself
becoming more beautiful within, and in turn that inward .
beauty will express itself in the outward form. Most true
artists are themselves beautiful to look upon, though it is
true that caricaturists are themselves caricatures, and fad-
dists look the part. If you contemplate the beauty of a
glorious sunset, or the magnificence of the splendid Himâlaya
mountains, or the grand rock and mountain masses of Rio de
Janeiro, you will find afterwards that their beauty and

strength have flowed into you, and you are more peaceful and firm than you were before. The stability and serenity of God have somehow entered into you, and poised your life within, making it serene and strong.

Just as the pursuit of knowledge develops the mind, so does the production of beauty through skilled action make the doer beautiful in his own form and movement. So, indeed, in every path does man approach God only by becoming God ; and on this line the real beauty is of the one who makes it. That is why beauty can never be superficial, nor can it be achieved through unbeautiful processes, any more than a structure of knowledge can be erected without truth in every part. Those who seek outward beauty, content to leave rubbish behind the scenes, are like those who imagine that great physical riches can give a life of strength and power, though their possessor be not himself strong in the riches of true human character. A horse runs well ; there is skill in action, real yoga—and what beauty in every movement of the whole and of every part, of every tiniest muscle ! So it is with all actions that ages of evolution or much training have perfected, and this is revealed to us more than ever to-day with the aid of slow-motion kinematography.

In those beautiful actions the philosopher or scientist may detect the stability of the principle of beauty, though the artist himself may not be specially interested in this aspect of the matter. There is the poise of balance in motion which is as truly stable as the splendid form of even a grand piece of modern Finnish architecture, and looking upon these things every man will say : " Yea, though I go to the highest heaven, I must take these things at least with me." It was with a true sense that the Pauranic writers lined the road to Yama's blessed city with horses that were descended from Uchchaihshrava and elephants of the family of Airâvata, and ducks on beautiful ponds and rivers, and great trees giving luscious shade. Beauty is the repose of perfect action in sound or color or form, and well has it been said that of all things in the material world art alone endures. Of it we may repeat Sir Edwin Arnold's beautiful words about the law of work, which shows the greatest skill in action :

> This is its touch upon the blossomed rose,
>   The fashion of its hand shaped lotus-leaves ;
> In dark soil and the silence of the seeds
>   The robe of Spring it weaves ;
>
> That is its painting on the glorious clouds,
>   And these its emeralds on the peacock's train
> It hath its stations in the stars ; its slaves
>   In lightning, wind and rain.
>
> Out of the dark it wrought the heart of man,
>   Out of dull shells the pheasant's pencilled neck ;
> Ever at toil, it brings to loveliness
>   All ancient wrath and wreck.
>
> The grey eggs in the golden sun-bird's nest
>   Its treasures are, the bees' six-sided cell
> Its honey-pot ; the ant wots of its ways,
>   The white doves know them well.
>
> The ordered music of the marching orbs
>   It makes in viewless canopy of sky ;
> In deep abyss of earth it hides up gold,
>   Sards, sapphires, lazuli.
>
> Ever and ever fetching secrets forth,
>   It sitteth in the green of forest-glades
> Nursing strange seedlings at the cedar's root,
>   Devising leaves, blooms, blades.

It is impossible to mention beauty without speaking of Japan. I have travelled the world over, and lived among people of twenty countries, but nowhere else have I seen the abundant beauty that fills the life of man in that land. The temples and gardens and art stores are among the wonders of the world, which no words can begin to describe, and one sees the value of the nation to humanity when one realises that every soul that passes through birth within it is inevitably touched with a sense of beauty far beyond what he had before. In other countries only rare souls are artistic, and they are lost and without much power amidst the rest ; but here everything is beautiful and the whole nation is touched. It is not for foreign visitors that their rarest pictures and objects of artcraft are made, but for themselves, and in the average home there is always the shrine of beauty in the principal living room—a recess the size of a door and several inches deep, with a little step to raise it from the floor. There are placed a few art treasures—one picture, the kakemono, and one piece of bronze or ivory or lacquer work or something of the kind, standing on a small ebony table or pedestal. On your first visit to the home you might think that these were all your friend's possessions, but later on you will find a different set of treasures in the shrine of beauty ? The lady of the house does not fill her rooms with beautiful things ; she understands the principle of beauty and keeps her collection in a closet, and shows but a few at one time. Where else do you find this understanding ? Even the lightest touch of the Japanese finger on the smallest thing makes it beautiful, with a beauty that is more literal than suggestive, for the seventh sub-race quality is so perfected that it almost hides the fourth root-race character in which it inheres. What other people will go out in their hundreds of thousands to admire their cherry blossom trees, which are grown for the blossom, not for the cherries, which are quite unfit to eat ? And where else will you find children treated with such rare gentleness, and taught to smile especially when they are in trouble, not to hearten themselves, but so that they may not convey their sorrows to others ? Such beauty and devotion to beauty are surely dear to the devas. Beauty, beauty, everywhere, and people supremely gentle, but of iron will.

A curious side expression of this principle, operating
through the sense of touch, is the instinct for cleanliness of
people of this ray. This is something different from neatness
or tidiness, and is akin to the removal of excrescences that
can release the beauty hidden in external things. The
Japanese exhibit this quality, for in the name of cleanliness
they almost boil themselves alive every day. It is not easy
to be too clean oneself, yet one recollects in this connection
the Japanese proverb about the fate of the fussy housewife
who tried to wash the tiger's face!

Ceremonial is also a very important part of the active
work of this ray, and might be described as the magic of it
practised by man. If you were living in a house where dwelt
a man of great and holy thought, you would be uplifted
by his thought-waves and thought-forms playing upon you
all the time, in so far as you could respond. It is the
experience of many pupils of the Masters, that in the
presence of their Teachers they can realise truths of which
they are uncertain at other times. The play of every kind of
kriyâshakti in the world is a very real thing. This power
operates through beauty as well as in other ways, and that it
is which transforms the pilgrim to Badarînârâyan into the
strength and purity of the Himâlayas themselves, and the
pilgrim to Kyoto into the sweetness of the gardens amid
which his shrines are set. Especially is all this true and
fruitful when the pilgrim is in reverent mood, for then he is
in a condition to respond to the power and absorb it with all
three parts of his personal constitution—body, feelings and
ideas. Ceremonial worship in every place and land lends
itself especially to the transmission of this influence; hence
beauty has come to mean very much in connection with
ceremony—beauty of odor, sound, color, form and movement, and without it many people cannot enjoy the fullest
amount of devotion that is possible for them.

15

So prominent a thing is ceremonial on the seventh ray that in India there are many people who when you speak of the path of action will think of the ceremonial forms in their religion, regarding those as the works that can bring man into touch with the devas, and believing that the service of the unseen in this manner brings upon them and their surroundings much uplifting grace. All this has been made an instrument for the deliberate helping of man, as in their different ways have all other things in which men's minds are definitely turned to some ideal, and for this purpose the great helpers of humanity have joined with the beauty of the ceremonial and its appeal to the devas the magic and symbology of the fourth ray. Thus we find in good ceremonial beautiful forms made manifoldly beautiful by beautiful thoughts that have been poured into them for centuries, also forms of deeply hidden beauty embodying the essential mathematics of the world, and the influence of the great deva kingdoms who live in the emotion of beauty and delight to be present wherever its forms may be found.

Among the animals, the cat well illustrates the qualities of the seventh ray. It is a creature in every part graceful, and beautiful in rest or in motion. There is a clumsiness of the horse and of the elephant, and even of the monkey and the dog, outside their special lines of development, but none for the cat whate'er befall. A friend of mine tells the story of a cat that lived next door to her, and used frequently to come into her house, apparently with a set purpose. It would quite regularly walk into the room where the people were sitting; if it found that they had a fire it would come right in and make itself at home, but if not it would despondently depart. The cat's love of luxury is not exactly love of ease, as in idle men, but is the gratification of sensitiveness ; it is the creature entering most fully into physical conditions, and inclined to be aloof with persons not because it does not like them but because its attention is otherwise engrossed. It is the animal that must have everything nice, that can keep itself clean, that cares more for house than persons, whom it values only for stroking and rubbing purposes ; and in turn it is loved by humankind not so much for the feelings of companionship that it shows as because it is beautiful to see and touch.

CHAPTER XVIII

A MASTER'S TABLE

Ray	Characteristic of Ray	Characteristic Magic	Last Religion
1	Fohat-Shechinah		Brahmanical
2	Wisdom	Raj Yog (Human Mind)	Buddhism
3	Akasa	Astrology (Natural Magnetic Forces)	Chaldean
4	Birth of Horus	Hatha Yog (Physical Development)	Egyptian
5	Fire	Alchemy (Material Substances)	Zoroastrian
6	Incarnation of Deity	Bhakti (Devotion)	Christianity, etc. (Kabala, etc.)
7		Ceremonial Magic	Elemental Worship

The above table of the rays is in the nature of an historical document. It was given to the famous occultist, C. W. Leadbeater, forty years ago at Adyar by the Master Djwâl Kûl, who told him, and the friends who were with him at the time, that that was all that it was then permissible to disclose to the world about the rays. It was not very intelligible at the time, but it has formed the classic foundation for further information that has been obtained from time to time. It now appears in his remarkable new book, *The Masters and the Path*. It first came into my hands only a few days ago, after I had written down all the ideas that are embodied in the foregoing chapters. Yet on looking it over I find that there is nothing in it to suggest any error in that work, or to hint at any necessary alteration. I am reproducing it here, with the permission of the author, because I think that my comments upon it may be interesting to students of the rays, and may help to elucidate some of the more obscure terms (such as " Birth of Horus ") which have been somewhat of a puzzle to many.

1. The words Fohat and Shechinah, which are put together to indicate the characteristic of the first ray will be familiar to students of Madame Blavatsky's great work, *The Secret Doctrine*. Fohat alone would indicate the perfectly indescribable power residing in the Universal God before manifestation, which was employed in some perfectly unthinkable manner when the unmanifested One willed to become many, and performed the self-change into two and three incident to that; but Fohat-Shechinah means the same power outward turned as Shakti, the first cause of manifested variety, appearing down at the level of man as the will in him—the faculty or power with which he changes himself, and so directs matter through mind, as I have already explained. It is true life attending to life, and causes the development of everything that grows. Occultists who have

had the rare fortune to see the Lord of the World, the Head of the First Ray of our globe, will link with this idea the memory of the electric character of His aura, that is like blue lightning, for He is the greatest active will and wielder of this power on our planet.

The table lists the characteristic magic of each ray. Why the Master should have spoken about magic in particular one cannot be sure, but we may speculate. The chief reason why knowledge about the rays has been disclosed so cautiously by the Adept Brotherhood was stated by Madame Blavatsky, when she said that knowledge of the rays gave great power. Many persons have been seeking it in order to find out their own rays, and then take up the appropriate magic, into which the force naturally coming through them might be expected to flow with great power and comparative ease. So the thought of magic was much in mind when the rays were spoken of. No magic is mentioned in connection with the first ray, because in all probability the will of the man himself, without any resort to other channels, was ever all the magic that the proud beings of this ray would condescend to employ, and surely their attitude is justified, since they feel the power of the self and can use it as no others may.

Every one who is directly acquainted with the Hindu or Brâhmanical religion, especially those forms of it which existed before the cult of Shrî Krishna arose, is impressed by its insistence upon the doctrine that the âtman or self in man is one with the universal self, an impregnable centre of consciousness, destined to win liberation from all earthly bonds not by any external grace, but by one-pointed mastery of every shred of his own being, and the unflinching assertion in thought and activity that is embodied in the great saying: "I am That." If that religion was not as soft or gentle in its earlier forms as it is at the present day, at least it presented in the strongest possible light, in its great doctrines of karma and dharma, the belief in the principle and value of justice, and the assertion that man has nothing to fear from outside himself, because he is divine and is the master of his own destiny.

The courage and will of the grandsire Bhîshma were typical of this religion. It was shown in his splendid independence; when threatened by King Shishupâla in terrible anger, he drew himself up and replied with great calm: " Know that I regard all the kings of the earth as lightly as a straw. If I be killed like a beast of the field or burnt to death, whatever may result, here do I put my foot upon all your heads. Before us now stands the Lord, whom I have worshipped." It is not necessary, I may say in passing, for first ray aspirants to imitate this language—the circumstances were extremely provoking, and besides, imitation is no characteristic of the first ray. Later on, on the field of combat, when Bhîshma lay dying, pierced with arrows and covered with wounds, he postponed his death to talk to the people gathering round of the value of the thirteen forms of truth, and to assure them that exertion is greater than destiny, and that the will of man is superior to all events. Even Shrî Krishna, who brought the second ray influence of love into greater prominence in Hinduism, begins His list of the divine qualities to be developed by men with the vigorous virtues of fearlessness, sâttvic purity, and the steadfast pursuit of wisdom.

2. The term wisdom, given as the characteristic of the second ray, needs little comment, but I must allude once more to the important fact already described at length that the active form and essence of all wisdom is love. The term râja yoga in the table applies, I think, to the splendid royal science of union taught in *The Bhagavad-Gîtâ* by Shrî Krishna, and the expression " human mind " used forty years ago in

this connection points not so much to the principle of manas the mind which in that râja yoga is considered to be only a sixth sense, as to that true centre of human consciousness which Theosophists call buddhi. The Buddhist religion is certainly typical of the second ray. How often its Founder, wandering up and down the valley of the Ganges, pointed out to the Hindus the danger of pride that lay in their doctrine of the self, should any man say: " I am That," thinking " I " as men are apt to do, in terms of matter or even of common consciousness. How often He emphasised that there was no eternal self such as men commonly thought the self to be. Remember, too, His teaching of kindliness—this Man " who made our Asia mild," and so impressed the quality of His wide love upon the world that the tens of thousands of millions of people, who have been His followers during the intervening centuries, have been noted above all others for their gentleness and lack of personal greed. It has been the one religion never to propagate itself by persecution ; yet it has won the greatest number of adherents that any religion has ever had. Surely this religion is of the second ray.

3. The characteristic of the third ray is given in the table as akâsha. Akâsha is the storehouse of the universal mind, the place of all archetypes, the first plane of matter on which operates the kriyâ or thought-power of our solar Logos. It is the great memory of the consciousness of our globe. It is the means by which consciousness fills space. From it by differentiation come all the phenomena of objective life. The term astrology, I believe, here relates not so much to the system of symbols and speculative correspondences that is called by that name to-day, as to the positive science of the influences of the Planetary Spirits who stand at the heads of rays. The man of this ray in learning his magic would get to know all about the characteristics of the seven distinctive types of every grade and kind of force and matter, so that

the whole world would be laid out for the expert on this ray as a great chess board on which he could see the powers and positions of all the pieces and adapt them to the purpose in hand in service of life. All the forces of nature form a great mathematical science, and they have their affinities, to which the term magnetic may very well be ascribed. The Chaldean religion with its elaborate astrolatry and practical astrology, its *Book of Numbers*, its linking of the tree of knowledge with the tree of life, and its great reverence for the moon god, seems naturally enough to have belonged to this ray.

4. We come next to the Birth of Horus, which looks very singular as the characteristic of a ray: but all becomes clear when we remember what has been said in Chapter VIII about mâyâ as an incarnation of Shiva, providing a link between Vishnu and Brahmâ, and introducing harmony into the relations between consciousness and matter. When Osiris was dispossessed of his kingdom the sufferings of the people became very great under their cruel oppressor, but he was reborn in his own son Horus, who came to avenge the wrongs and restore happiness. In the Egyptian religion the ceremonial mourning for the death of Osiris was a very real grief, and it typified the great hunger for happiness (our ânanda) which people are everywhere seeking in earthly bonds. Set, the murderer of Osiris, the rebellious elements of nature, and the darkness of night, was defeated by Horus, who restored harmony and ultimately became the God of just rewards and punishments. Horus, too, was typical of man, the being in the midmost state, in whom the highest spirit and the lowest matter find their meeting-ground, and have their conflict and harmony.

As this is a subject of very great interest I will endeavor to explain it more fully by reference to the seven principles in man. The fourth principle is what is sometimes called antahkarana, which means literally the internal cause or

16

instrument or agency. Above it (in a sense) we have âtmâ, buddhi and manas, representing the first three principles, and below it we have three principles which represent in the human constitution the fifth, sixth and seventh. The terms used for describing these last three have become exceedingly confused, having been used by different authors in different ways. Let me prescribe a set of terms for the convenience of our present study. What is commonly called the lower mind is kâma-manas, that is, manas with desire, manas taking an interest in external things. Perhaps the word kâma has been used in too limited a sense, to imply nothing but gross sensual desire, but it means all desire. And desire is the outward-turned aspect of love, the love of the *things* of the three worlds; while love proper is love of life or love of the divine, and belongs to the higher or inward-turning self. What is commonly called the astral principle is simply kâma, though it becomes kâma-rupa when a definite astral body is formed. The seventh principle is in the etheric double, which was sometime called the linga sharîra or subtle body.

The dense physical body has no real principle of man in it. It is just a part of the external world. It is not even the hand of the man, but it is a tool held in his hand, which is the etheric double. The dense body is only employed to carry about the interior organs in which the man really functions on the physical plane. In tables of the seven principles, some show the antahkarana and others the dense physical body, but none of them lists both together. We may make three tables, as follows:

1	2	3
1. Atmâ	1. Atmâ	4. Monad
2. Buddhi	2. Buddhi	1. Atmâ
3. Manas	3. Manas	2. Buddhi
5. Lower manas (kâma-manas)	4. Antahkarana	3. Manas
6. Astral (kâma-rupa)	5. Kâma-manas	5. Kâma-manas
7. Etheric (linga-sharîra)	6. Kâma-rupa	6. Kâma-rupa
4. Physical body	7. Linga-sharîra	7. Linga-sharîra

As will be seen presently, the first table rightly gives the seven principles of the ordinary man, the second table gives those of the occultist who has not reached perfection, and the third table gives those of the Adept at the moment of his attainment. The principle which we are now studying operates through the physical body in the first case, through the antahkarana in the second, and through the monad in the third.

Now, there is a wonderful connection between the monad, the antahkarana, and the physical body; but as this is slightly difficult to grasp, I will lead up to it gradually. The âtmâ-buddhi-manas is the divine in man. It is that part of man which really evolves—especially the causal body receives an impetus on the probationary path, the buddhic on the first half of the Path proper (between the First and the Fourth Initiations), and the âtmic on the second half of that Path (between the Fourth and Fifth Initiations). Its prime business is therefore on these planes, but it needs something to specialise its functions, like the speck of dust in the fog or like the bit of dirt in the pearl. Later, too, it will have to become a Logos, so it must learn to see a world from that world's inside, that is to say from its own outside. Hence the necessity for its immersion in matter.

The divine cannot enter the material worlds, therefore, all at once, but only point by point. The antahkarana joining it to a given personality he is such a point. The antahkarana is thus a substitute in the lower man for the higher self. In a given incarnation the higher self has no intention to exhibit itself and all that it has acquired of development in previous lives. Something has been selected for a special purpose for this life, and the personality will have to be content not to evolve itself, but to do the lesson of the moment. It is a creature of the present, not of eternity. That is why it must give itself up utterly to the higher, with absolutely no hope of anything for itself, except its reward in devachan. If it does not do this, it becomes the opponent of the higher, the thwarter of its purpose.

All this was indicated in the Egyptian story of Osiris. The higher self is Osiris. Osiris has his work to do in the higher fields. He cannot stay below to wage war with Typhon or Set, but he provides a son, Horus, for the purpose. Horus is the antahkarana. The antahkarana is the only thing that is divine in the personality, and it is a small incarnation of its own father. This explains the term "Birth of Horus".

Next, let us observe the distinction between the personality and the set of bodies. Horus ought to be the ruler of the personality. That is to say, he ought to build a kingdom on earth that will represent his father. In such a case the bodies would attract kinds of matter, acquire rates of vibration, and establish forms and habits, consistent with a personality from above. Horus would then be the divine personality in man, entirely in harmony with the three higher principles, established in a kingdom on earth as it is in heaven, and the divine tetractys (of one kind) would have been formed.

But there is karma to be dealt with—the karma of the actions done through the dense physical body in previous incarnations. That karma enters in to give shape to that body from the outside, through heredity and other agencies, even before it is born. Outside things are constantly battering upon it in multitudinous ways from the moment of its birth, and they tend to build up another sort of personality. Typhon wants to be the ruler. If he should win the battle to a large extent in any incarnation and take Horus prisoner we have then the most unhappy phenomenon of the establishment of "self-personality".

Still, even that defeat is not for nothing. If the higher is not yet able to be master amid the experiences that past

karma brings, it only indicates that it is still in a state of
tuition, not of intuition. It must learn by experience—sometimes by bitter experience. But all the experience that
karma brings is good for the evolution of the soul, and though
it may come in the guise of an enemy, it is really the best
of friends. Therefore at last Typhon is no enemy, but is
another substitute—a substitute for the antahkarana, providing an orderly continuum of training for the higher, a means
of continuing its growth. It is the representative of the
kârmic Lords.

Now we come to the crux of the matter. I have said
that the antahkarana is a substitute for the divine, the higher
self. It is not quite true, yet it seemed to have to be said,
that we might be led on to the deeper truth. The divine is
the subject of experience, the one who experiences ; the
material is the object. These two cannot come together by
means of anything that is in either of them ; but they do get
together because they are both abstractions from a greater
whole. Let us recall the story of the Pillar of Light. Vishnu
(the Second Logos, the Divine) and Brahmâ, (the Third
Logos, the Material) could not get along together, until
Shiva (the First Logos) appeared and proved to them that
He was utterly superior to both of them. Then both became
devoted to Him and began to work together in obedience to
Him. He would not stay with them, however, but He
established harmony between them, and promised that they
should see Him again when their work was finished. The
harmony remained, a means of connection between the
subject and the object, the knower and the known, the divine
and the material. That harmony is mâyâ ; it is our life,
which is a substitute for the real life.

In the human being the antahkarana is thus the representative of mâyâ, and so again is the physical body,
which is the fulcrum of karma. And since the monad is

the First Logos in man, the higher self the Second (with three faculties), and lower self the Third (also with three qualities), the antahkarana represents that First Logos (the monad) until the joint work of the Third and the Second Logos is completed. When that is done, the antahkarana is no longer necessary, for the man has completed his human career, and they are in the presence of their Lord (the monad) again. Thus on the attainment of Adeptship the antahkarana ceases to be necessary, as even the ego then becomes only an instrument; consciousness is no longer the man himself, but only a set of powers.

Hatha yoga is given as the magic of this ray. In India it is based upon the theory of correspondences, and the belief that just as the mind influences the body, so does the body influence the mind. Its votaries practise the most rigid control of the body, not by the infliction of any torments or injuries upon it, except among some ignorant and superstitious followers of the cult, but to bring it into the most perfect condition of physical health and endurance, and operate upon the etheric double by systems of breathing —all in order to achieve mind-powers or siddhis, or to obtain great concentration. The Egyptian magic took into account not only the body but a great variety of things, and working through symbology and correspondences produced effects in the inner and outer worlds. Everything external seems to have had to them a significance and effect internally, so closely did they link together the inner and outer worlds in their thought, and in their lives as well.

5. On the fifth ray we find fire mentioned as the characteristic, and alchemy as the magic. This points very clearly to the scientific ray, on which the most scrupulous truth and purity are requisite for success. Agni, or fire in all its forms, has had much to do with man's work in chemistry and physics and every other branch of pure and applied science.

It is connected with the concrete mind of man, and also with
the very interesting fact that science depends almost entirely
upon the sense of sight and therefore the agency of light, a
form of agni. If, for example, knowledge is required about
the nature of the heat in a body, the scientist does not touch
it with his finger in order to get to know about the heat by
feeling ; he employs a thermometer to indicate the heat in a
visible manner. As every one knows, Zoroastrianism is the
religion of fire and of purity.

6. Ray six has the characteristic " incarnation of deity,"
and as its means of magical power, bhakti or devotion. This
agrees exactly with our scheme, for the devotee of this ray
looks to God as goodness incarnate in the objective world,
not to the abstract deities more attractive to men of other
rays. Christianity has always been for the most part a
religion of this type, not unmindful of riches and prosperity
on earth and in the life to come.

7. For some reason unknown the seventh ray characteristic was not given, possibly because had beauty been mentioned, its deep-seated character might have been overlooked.
All accounts of man's relations with the great deva evolution
show how dear to those beings is everything that is beautiful, in nature and in art, in form, color, and sound and in
every other way. Particularly has it been considered that
delightful odors are pleasing and attractive to them. That
ceremonial should be the magic of this ray is not unnatural
under these circumstances, and the gorgeous colors and
sounds and rhythmic motions which nearly always accompany
it can improve the psychic environment or atmosphere for
humanity by bringing the devas closer into touch with us.
Sensitiveness to the existence of invisible beings in nature
led also to the earlier forms of this activity, in which men
contacted nature spirits and devas through suitable ceremonial forms.

PART III

THE GREAT USE AND DANGER

OF

KNOWLEDGE OF THE RAYS

"O wise man, remove the conception that Not-Spirit is Spirit"—says Shankaracharya. Atma is Not-Spirit in its final Parabrahmic state; Ishvara, or Logos, is Spirit; or, as Occultism explains, it is a compound unity of manifested living Spirits.

THE SECRET DOCTRINE.

Though Ishvara is "God"—unchanged in the profoundest depths of Pralayas and in the intensest activity of Manvantaras, still beyond him is ATMA, round whose pavilion is the darkness of eternal MAYA.

THE SECRET DOCTRINE.

CHAPTER XIX

YOUR RAY

THIS knowledge about the rays is only for those who have an ideal, a star shining in the East, attracting them with irresistible fascination, so that they cannot but make their way towards it as their path in life. Others, who live still for the momentary satisfaction of the body and the senses and the mind, are yet the servants of mâyâ, and they have such changing pleasures as the animals enjoy. But only he who has a constant ideal is on the way to the real life which is ânanda, happiness, and even then, if he is to tread the road swiftly, he will need not only the guiding star of his ideal, shining far above and before him in the darkness of the night, but also a lamp of virtue for his feet, and a power to move his limbs. Still more, to tread it with the greatest speed he must determine which star he is destined to follow and what virtue and power must be his, or in other words, he must find out his ray.

This is only possible when his life is managed from within. The other day I watched two chess-players. One was bending over the board with anxious eye and furrowed brow, and his fingers trembled as he made his moves ; the other was leaning back, calmly studying the board, and when he touched the pieces it was with natural and inconspicuous grace. He who would tread the path to happiness must realise that life is such a game and nothing more. It lies in the meeting place of two worlds. Let us call the place where I meet the outside world " my world ". It is not the whole of the world, but only that part of it in which my game is going on, where things touch and stir me through the senses and I influence them by my thought. Many things there are in time and space that will not touch me in the course of the present game, and many things there are beyond the reach of my powers ; but certain it is that there is a region that is " my world," larger or smaller according to the extent to which I have gone out to the world and taken it into my hands, or have entered on the game of life.

All the pieces on this board are things for use—king, queen, bishops, knights, rooks and pawns—family, wealth. fame, friends, business connections—and even the body, with its qualities of health and strength in organ and limb, sense and brain, and its habits physical, emotional and mental. The game goes on for you in your world, the meeting place of the hidden self and the greater world. At first your position is safe, but you make a move to enlarge or enjoy your powers, and at once are open to attack. For every move of yours there is a move in reply, in the world where action and reaction are inseparable. Good positions, bad positions, come and go ; pawns and knights fall, but you have not fallen, and you learn to value the pieces only for their use, and calmly let them go when by their sacrifice a better position may be achieved. Down they go, bishop and rook and queen, but you are not down. And you are not lost even when the king himself is gone, the very body that is your last piece on the board. It is no matter for regret, for if you have played the game well you will be stronger for the next.

The events of life never really touch you, but only affect your world. Bend over in anxiety, full of unwisdom, and it will seem that the loss of pawn or rook is an injury to the very self, but in reality nothing of it has touched you, but

only your world, and all events are favorable to the
calm and active soul. Sit up and lean back, and you shall
see it so.

I would define five stages in the progress or evolution of
the human soul, and everywhere men are to be seen on
different rungs of this ladder:

    Stage 1. Leaning back.
        „   2. Sitting up.
        „   3. Bending over.
        „   4. Sitting up.
        „   5. Leaning back.

The first stage is that of the primitive and unawakened
man, whether civilised or not, sluggish and uninterested,
moved to activity only by the strong blows of fate. The
second is that of the man who has learned that the world
contains things of great delight, and he is full of eagerness for
them, even to the extent of greed. In the third stage he is
still filled with eager desire, but has found that the world is
full of dangers and compensations, and has definite laws of
its own, and he is anxious to steer the frail vessel of his
existence safely through the rapids of life. In the fourth
stage the man is still immersed in the game, but he is playing
it with dignity, even though he feels keenly every gain and
loss; but in the fifth he plays the game as one who is immortal, who knows and feels all the time that at last he cannot
but win in the greater game of which this is a little part, because he is growing stronger all the time. He is released
from anxiety, discontent and resentment; for him hope and
fear are gone, and he cannot throw himself upon the mercy
of events so as to wish that his opponent should move as he
desires. Whatever happens he does not lose his calm; he
plays the game leaning back upon himself, as it were, and his
sleeping strength is like that behind the tiger's spring. As
other people have distinguished their universe of experience

into two practical parts, " myself and the world," he has distinguished it into three practical parts, "myself," "my world," and "the world ". Now he has nothing to fear from the world, but only from himself, and his only care is to be watchful to use his powers and never let them sleep.

Having gained this position, in some measure, the question is : how may you find out what is your ray ? It is impossible to lay down any rules by means of which this discovery can be made, but there are certain questions which you may put to yourself which will assist the descent of intuition into the brain. You may have strong inclinations for learning or philanthropy or art at the present time, but they may be but a passing phase, an interest stimulated by environment. First ask yourself in what way the cramping limitations were removed from your soul's need by the great Theosophical science. (1) Did it seem to open up an endless path of victory for the triumphant progress of the aspiring soul ? (2) Did it seem to remove the obstacles to the universal expansion of the sunny heart ? (3) Did it remove the confusion from a mind that wanted to grasp everything in one all-embracing plan ? (4) Did it show that there were spiritual purposes even in the darkest spots of life, and that even in perfection all the imperfect things would also have a rightful place ? (5-7) Did it promise you time and opportunity for the perfection of knowledge, or an endless vista of contact with all that could be conceived as most glorious, or the certainty of ultimate consummate skill in an art which even all your lifelong energy must leave short of full achievement ? Dwell upon these things utterly without desire that your ray should be this one or that one, and intuition may speak.

Again you may ask yourself, looking backwards, what has been your influence on others. That may tell you something, since every man gives what he has, and nothing else. Did you leave them stronger than before and more able to face the adventure of life on account of their contact with you? Did you awaken them to a greater sensibility of the life other than their own that pervades the world? Did you cause them to understand from within themselves the mystery of being? And all these things even without thought to do it on your part, just because you were there? And also how has the world taught you.? If through experience bearing clear and definite lessons, probably you have acted first and thought afterwards in your past; but if the world has placed things gently before you for your own choosing and consideration, probably the reverse was the case.

Above all, what do you want deep down inside yourself? Put aside all your desires, and ask yourself what it is that you really want, and do not accept any superficial answer, but ask yourself why you give that answer and what is the deeper need that remains behind. If you have liking or dis-liking, a passing and superficial fancy or repugnance, for any of the rays, it will distort your vision of the truth. You must be absolutely willing to accept anything from the intuition, and never question it while hoping that its answer may be this or that.

Once more, you may narrow the field of enquiry by con-sidering the three powers of the mind; in their councils which is the proposer of most of the resolutions, and which urges the others into active being? Do you seek knowledge and power because of love that makes you want to serve God or to help your fellow-men? Do you seek the company of others and the opportunities of life for the sake of understanding? Or is it the vigor of the self who, being, must live fully, that sends you into the melée of life because life is life, and is to be lived abundantly? Again, when you look deep within, do you find a relentless purpose, a constant pushing onward; do you find an unshrinking love, ever ready to embrace the lives of others; do you find an unceasing longing for the spotless truth?

Test yourself again by your failures. There are three great spiritual laws which no true man should ever disobey; he must be awake and active with his powers; he must be true to himself and others, and full of love. If he seeks the highest it is inexcusable and unjustifiable, (but all the same he will do it, but less and less as time goes on) to sacrifice at any time one of these principles for the sake of another, amid the conflicts of duty in practical life. In the past which have you sacrificed? Has it been in order to be kind that you have been untruthful, or that in your faithfulness to truth you have caused pain, or that in pushing forward to success some work that was well intentioned and seemed to you vitally important, you have permitted some laxity in truth or love by the way? The principle to which you held may indicate your ray. And again, are you most prone to pride, anger or fear? But all these things are only of uncertain assistance, because the knowledge must come from within.

It is also necessary in this endeavor to discern your ray not to compare yourself with others. It may be that you are much feebler in understanding than many other people whom you know, and yet that it is the strongest thing in your character, the other principles being feebler still. It may be, too, that one person's ray is love, and yet his will may be stronger than that of another who belongs even to the first ray. The question is not how you stand as compared with any other person, but what principle is the leader of the forces within your own soul. The perfect man in the weakest of these principles is as strong as the still imperfect man in his strongest, for he has achieved in all of them all that is possible for anyone living in a human form.

When you have chosen your guiding star, the following will be the lamps to light your feet through the tangled undergrowth of life, and the powers that will speed you on your way :

Ray	Star	Lamp	Power	Work
1.	Freedom	Courage	Will	Government
2.	Union	Love	Love	Philanthropy
3.	Comprehension	Truth	Thought	Philosophy
4.	Harmony	Courage	Imagination	Interpretation
5.	Truth	Truth	Thought	Science
6.	Goodness	Love	Love	Religion
7.	Beauty	Courage	Will	Art

The issue is sometimes further complicated by the presence in the character of a strong second principle. Of course, every ray has its seven subdivisions, and each of those its seven again, but those we are not considering, because within a principle the characteristics of that principle are dominant over all these shades, just as all shades of yellow are yellow, and all shades of green are green. But it may be that the second strongest principle in one's constitution has a voice of its own clear and strong, and under some circumstances of life almost as prominent as the first. Different ideas have been attached to the term sub-ray, but here I want to use it to indicate this principle second in strength.

CHAPTER XX

PROGRESS WITHOUT DANGER

THE object of our life at the present stage is to develop our consciousness, or rather our conscious powers, to human perfection, and this knowledge of the rays is supremely useful to that end. When a man knows what his ray is, he has discovered his strongest power. When he uses that strongest power he will move forward very rapidly, with glorious or disastrous results as the case may be. It is largely because of the great danger involved, which cannot easily be overestimated, that knowledge about the rays has been kept back until those who are likely to receive it have learned a good deal about the nature of human life and the reality of brotherhood. If a man is filled with one ideal and he identifies his life with that and feels the power of it in him, he is tempted to drive along on that one line and neglect his weaknesses, and in all such cases the effort to progress is almost sure to end in a crash. How that comes about may be sufficiently illustrated with one or two simple examples. If it is the truth that the man is seeking, on the scientific ray. and there is little love or devotion in his nature, the aspirant will soon be capable not only of animal, but of human experimentation. If, again, the person is capable of philanthropy, and pursues that line with great power, but is lacking in both kinds of intelligence, he may without intending it do most foolish things in his zeal for the welfare of mankind, and even precipitate revolution and bloodshed if he has power enough.

The great use of this knowledge about the rays is that you should find and feel your power, and then employ it to the utmost to develop the other qualities in yourself that are relatively deficient. Readers of my little book *Character Building* will remember that all strong human vices indicate a deficiency of character in company with certain strength. A character that is weak in all respects has not the power to do anything much, and such a person is usually classed as a good man, though it would be difficult to say what he is good for. If therefore a man finds he has some positive defect, he need not try to suppress his power, and say: "I have too much feeling, or too much energy, or too much will." Let him say: "I have great will-power, but a poor set of human feelings, and I must use my will-power to compel myself to mingle with people and think of them and help them constantly, until my human emotions have reached a higher standard." In this case, and all similar ones, the man gains much but loses nothing, for he develops his will-power just as if he had been using it for selfish purposes, but he develops love at the same time. Of course, it is hard to change one's motives, but the man who realises that the purpose of human life is just character building, and who believes in reincarnation, will soon find that all smaller motives fade away, and that in doing his best for himself he is brought into the largest and most beneficial relations with other people.

The same principle may be applied in outward and social relations. The rays are not separate ladders on which men are climbing apart from one another. Together they form an organism. So the man of a given ray may be true to himself, using his own powers, working not to gratify his own ambitions, but to further the ends of others, provided they are good and of the soul. As eyes work for the convenience of hands and feet, and feet carry hands and eyes about, so may the scientist, as engineer and architect, build a temple for devotees, or an artist may design and equip the philosopher's den or garden.

On this path of progress towards perfect consciousness it is not necessary for a man to pay attention to all seven rays and attempt to perfect himself in every one of them. But he must strive to perfect himself in three—one expressing the power of will, another that of love, another that of thought. Thus if he is a good philosopher, he need not trouble about being proficient in science, or if he is strongly attached to the arts of the seventh ray, he need not specially trouble himself about the work of the first ray. For this purpose, however, he whose strongest principle is the fourth may consider that his deficiency lies in two or six, and three or five, rather than in one or seven, because there is a strong affinity between rays one, four and seven, as there is between two and six, and three and five.

It is advisable, however, in all cases, that one at least of the three chosen lines of self-training should be within the group of rays one to three, and that another one should be within the group five to seven; this will give a more perfect balance in the character, and will prevent the aspirant from being too much aloof from the world or too much immersed in it.

I have spoken of a man's second strongest principle as his sub-ray. If that secondary characteristic of his happens to be within the same group as his ray, as, for example, ray two and sub-ray three, or ray five and sub-ray seven, it will also tend to form an unbalanced character. In this case the man will be well advised to choose as his third quality to work upon one from the other group, and bring all the power of his ray to bear upon the development of that.

In choosing his three lines of training no one should do violence to his predilections. His ray quality ought to be his first selection and his second choice will probably be what I

have called his sub-ray, his second principle in strength, and
then he should choose what he likes best among what are left
when the rule that I have described has been applied. He
need not then fear to make the most rapid progress that he
can, always regarding the third selection as his weakest
point, and using his strongest power for the deliberate
development of that.

In order that swiftest progress may be made, it is
necessary also to understand the two great laws that are
constantly promoting it. Just as there are two ultimate
principles in the world of experience—the great active principle, Vishnu, and the great passive principle, Brahmâ—so there
are two great laws, called dharma and karma respectively,
which belong to them, and both these laws operate for the
development of consciousness.

The law of karma is often regarded as bestowing punishment upon those who have brought pain or difficulty to others,
but that does not describe its true character. It is really a
scheme in the harmony of things whereby a man is taught
from the outside what he neglects to learn by the use of the
powers of his consciousness. It is the way of nature to insist
that a man shall fulfil the responsibilities that he has
acquired by the development of his powers so far. I may
return to my simile of the game of chess. You have made
some moves and acquired a certain position, and you cannot
in fairness to your opponent decline to make another move
just because the game is not going as you like it, or because
you feel sleepy and want to give it up. You cannot be
passive, but must under penalty continue the game of life,
whose umpire will brook no dishonorable laxity on our part.
The world punishes idleness, selfishness and thoughtlessness,
and no degree of innocence will save a man from being run
over by a motor car if he persists in crossing Piccadilly or
Fifth Avenue with his eyes shut. That is the law of our

relation to this material world, and it is exactly the same as that which causes our hand to be burnt when we put it in the fire, and do not employ our intelligence to make our investigations into the nature of fire in a more discreet manner. There can therefore be no passivism ; every aspirant on this path must be prepared to pay attention to what the world specifically puts before him, and must believe that it contains a lesson specially intended for him and necessary for his further growth. Either by willing use of them in an active, unselfish and thoughtful life may a man develop his powers of will, love and thought, or else he will be taught forcibly, and with pain if need be, from the outside. Well was it said by Emerson :

> Every day brings a ship.
> Every ship brings a word;
> Well for those who have no fear,
> Looking seaward, well assured
> That the word the vessel brings
> Is the word they wish to hear.

It is also part of this law that a man shall receive the hurt or benefit that he has given to others, but this also is no punishment but purely education. A man who could intentionally injure another is himself insensitive to that other's feelings and welfare, and being thus insensitive he needs strong experience to make him feel ; or it may be that he has been thoughtlessly stupid, and once more needs decided experience to make him pay attention. There are few people who repent of their folly without this lesson. " Had I but served my God with half the zeal I served my king, he would not in mine age have left me naked to mine enemies," said Wolsey, and his method of learning was quite a typical case. The Cardinal not only suffered the stripes that he had given to others, but in doing so he also caught a glimpse of wisdom, a sight of what was desirable in life. It was no discredit to him that he could not see it till the world struck him hard ; that is the way of life. Indeed, the object of incarnation is not to enjoy the powers already won, but to develop those that are deficient, and the law of karma is always active in providing the external conditions which can best restore a balance to character. When it obstructs our doing what we want to do because we can do it easily and well, it is not an enemy, but a friend pointing out the true path of growth.

To make the greatest possible progress, then, a man must not only be willing to accept the game as he finds it on the board of life, and be ready to play it to the end, with whatever pieces there may be in whatever position they may be, but must do it with delighted acceptance and heartiest co-operation, not wishing that some other person's game were his. "Each man reaches perfection," says the *Gîtâ*, "by being intent upon his own karma."

The other law, dharma, is that of the evolution of consciousness, and there is really no other evolution, since the forms of nature are merely built round the evolving consciousness. A man's dharma is his position on the ladder of conscious evolution, and the main part of this law is that powers of love, will and thought grow by use and not otherwise. It is therefore wisdom for any man to employ his powers even if they be insignificant, instead of shrinking from their use because he cannot measure up to the standard of others whom he admires. No growth will come to him by waiting, nor by his trying to perform a task to which his powers are not adapted. Let us hear again *The Bhagavad-Gîtâ*: "Better is one's own dharma, though inglorious, than the successful dharma of another. He who doeth the karma prescribed by his own nature incurreth not sin."

It is one feature of the law of karma—man's relation to the world around him—that when he pursues the activity of one of the rays, he develops at the same time the quality of the corresponding ray. One who takes to the pursuit of beauty as an artist of any kind develops at the same time the will and self-control that mark the first ray. One who follows a path of devotion, let us say to the Christ, will be led into ever enlarging fields of human brotherhood. One who pursues the truth as a scientist will also become something of a philosopher. One who sets himself to do work with the greatest possible skill, that is to say, work with will behind it, will be led to an experience and interest in beauty, because as I have said before, skill in action is always beautiful as well as the cause of beauty; he who follows the feelings of human brotherhood may start with feelings of comradeship, but he will end by adding to them a devoted appreciation of those who are his superiors, elder brothers in the great human family. And the philosopher who seeks to understand man's relation to the world will find himself in the realm of science.

In the progress of nations also this is visible. The great scientific tendency of our present sub-race is constantly breaking out into philosophy and developing the higher mind; and it is already apparent in America, where people worship bounty and prosperity and are unstinted in their admiration of everything great, that the sixth sub-race mind is already feeling a great sense of brotherhood, as perhaps nowhere else in the world. When brotherhood has won its way in the world in the still distant maturity of that race, as science has achieved great triumphs and pervaded even the small details of home life in the fifth, all that will be left, one may predict, for men to do in the seventh race will be to make life beautiful in every way and every part, and doing that they will achieve great power of the will, and the enjoyment of the outward freedom that will make possible the enlightened anarchy that is impossible until brotherhood has played its part.

CHAPTER XXI

STAGES OF SELF-REALIZATION

" NEAR and proper to us," said Emerson, " is that old fable of the Sphinx, who was said to sit in the road-side and put riddles to every passenger. If the man could not answer, she swallowed him alive. What is our life but an endless flight of winged facts or events ? In splendid variety these changes come, all putting questions to the human spirit. Those men who cannot answer by superior wisdom these facts or questions of time, serve them. Facts encumber them, tyrannise over them, and make the men of routine, the men of *sense*, in whom a literal obedience to facts has extinguished every spark of that light by which man is truly man. But if the man is true to his better instincts or sentiments, and refuses the domination of facts, as one that comes of a higher race, remains fast by the soul and sees the principle, then the facts fall aptly and supply into their places ; they know their master, and the meanest of them glorifies him." This indicates, as I have said before, that man belongs to consciousness, and if he will positively stand by that he need fear nothing, and everything will go well with him. It is important, however, to realise what part of that which a man commonly thinks to be himself is in reality but a portion of the external world. Let us analyse the man and see.

First, there is a set of material bodies—the physical body, with its companions on subtler planes. This provides

19

a limiting instrument for the consciousness, and coming into
incarnation in it is distinctly an act of concentration. As I
have explained in my lecture on *Personal Psychology and the
Subconscious Mind,* the body is literally a camera—a dark
box. It shuts us away from the world. It does not present the
world to us, as is commonly supposed. The sense organs in
the body serve, however, to mitigate its function of obscuration to some extent. They admit a little light from the world
to the consciousness, and because of that there is a very clear
image on the screen of the mind. The vision belongs to
consciousness, never to the box; and that consciousness is
open to the world and capable of seeing the whole of it,
except as it has entered this camera, so as to concentrate
much of its attention upon one small beam of light. But the
consciousness open to the world has the vaguest and most
indefinite sense of it all—a great undeveloped, subconscious
mind it is, but with clear and brilliant parts in it, resulting
from those bright and vivid experiences that it has obtained
through the camera of the body.

A natural consequence of this is that in the body a man
deals with one thing after another; he does not evolve at all
in that body, and the body does not evolve, but it goes through
a series of changes like the seasons of the year, and is always
losing as well as gaining. It is not that the man of middle
age is perfect, and that the child is imperfect, and the old
man imperfect. The child and the aged man have their own
perfection that the mature man has not. It is similar, too,
to the experience of a child at school, who in the course of
the day takes half-a-dozen lessons on different subjects from
different teachers in different rooms. True it is that to-
morrow the child will go into those class rooms again and in
every one of them will learn more than it could on the preced-
ing day, because in the realm of knowledge "to him that
hath more shall be given" and the power of the mind increases

day by day. And equally true it is that, in future incarnations, as each one of us goes through the seasons of his life, he will fare better in each of them and be richer in consciousness. Then, as this enrichment proceeds, it will be possible for the sense organs of the bodies to be enlarged in their scope, as the consciousness growing stronger is able to take a bigger hold upon things, until at last it stands in its perfection, open to all the world, seeing without eyes and hearing without ears, ready to enter the transcendent state of Vishnu's consciousness.

But until that great day to this each embodied man must at last reconcile himself—that for himself as the person in the body there is no progress and no approach to perfection. While he is learning one thing in one class now, and giving full attention to that, what he learnt an hour ago in another class is very largely obscured. His business it is to live from hour to hour, making the best possible use of each. The very purpose of his incarnation is to gain something new; all the attention of his senses, feelings and thoughts is being given to that, and that portion of himself so engaged is clearly seen and felt as a thing among other things.

The second thing in our analysis is the personality. It is not the set of bodies, but something that has grown up with them. The little child, though it is feeling, and even thinking and willing, through the body, has at first no personality, but little by little it becomes involved in the third person and thinks "I am this," and as the years go on and the body grows up that becomes a very definite thing. The physical body has been trained in a certain manner and has acquired a set of habits; attached to it are sets of emotional and mental habits as well, inhering in the astral and mental bodies, and all this forms a distinct personality, reacting in a definite way to the world. That is not the man himself, and the right pronoun to apply to it is " it ".

That personality is or ought to be an instrument, something fine and good and strong and pure and definite, and useful especially for some distinct walk in life, whereby decided and valuable experience may be obtained through it. Yet it should be an instrument through which the man himself can think and love and will; not one set only in the habit of response to external things, but also open to the man within.

Let me take one illustration of this work. If a man, being a good writer or tennis player with his right hand, should compel himself to learn to write or play equally well with his left hand, we know that that would be a matter of benefit to him in several ways, and if we could imagine a personal man as living for a vast length of time in one body, we should say that those accomplishments would be worth his while as part of his perfecting. While he was learning to use his left hand he would be practising concentration, foregoing something while working for something else. Such is the way in incarnation; the true man is the right-handed skilful player, but the person must learn to make use of all his time; he may not spend his time in the enjoyment or display of that which has already been achieved; he must allow himself to be used for the gaining of new power by the man within. Under these circumstances any sort of personal ambition (sankalpa, it is called in Sanskrit), is bound to render him less useful to the inner man of conscious being and purpose.

If the personal man chooses to live from moment to moment, doing the work of the inner man, and living for his ideals, he is that real man, but if he imagines himself to be something on his own account, and develops a notion of becoming something more, he is doomed to sorrow. He must not have greed of any kind, not even for knowledge. In Bolivia the native and half-caste women show their social standing and their wealth by wearing as many skirts as possible all at once. Their form of grandeur does not uplift them, nor edify the beholders. The same thing is true also of the personality which strives to be a walking encyclopædia. What is needed for the personality is such riches and knowledge as will enable it to do the kind of work for which it is fitted in the world, and when one sees personalities assuming more than that, one is reminded of the Bolivian women and their skirts. What one sees in a nice dog or cat or horse or other creature is something of an ideal for the personality—without excrescences and ornaments, which may be all right in some other place, they can be beautiful indeed.

The third element in our analysis may be described as self-personality. If the consciousness in man has become submerged in that personality, thinking " I am this " to the exclusion of all else, then the personality usurps the throne of the self within, and the life is lived in the interests of its prolongation and its physical, emotional and mental comforts and ambitions. Then the man of ideals, the true man, is starved for the rest of that incarnation. Personality is a good thing, but self-personality is the greatest curse.

Our fourth item in the analysis is the conscious man, whose true interest in life is in the activities of one of the rays which I have described, in the pursuit of one of the ideals. Insomuch as he can destroy self-personality while keeping his personality strong will his incarnated life be fruitful. Each man may test himself. While he is full of his ideal all is well, but when he falls into self-personality he is lost. In testing this, let him ask himself not only what occupies his mind while he is thinking, but even more what does so when he is not. With arduous training and self-purification he will be able to produce in the personality such essential habits of emotion and thought that in its rest it will be open inwards rather than outwards, interested in ideals, not merely in personal things.

The pronoun that now applies to the man is " you ". He cannot be thought of as any objective thing ; to be known he must be felt as life, whether so felt by himself or by any other. In no other way can he be known. It is here that are to be found the collected fruits of the labors of the personality. Here is something that evolves in power so that in one incarnation it can hold in one handful (of will, or love or thought) and express in one act of being a number of things which in a previous incarnation it picked up with difficulty one by one. This " you " remains the same consciousness throughout all the material changes. A material thing cannot change and yet be the same, because of its space limitation, but this conscious " you " can so remain through a series of changes in which your thought and feeling and will have ever greater scope, and constantly grasp a greater portion of the material world.

And yet this consciousness in turn is not the " I," not even at the point of triumph when it stands beyond the need of human incarnation. I must learn to know it as " you," one of the many " yous " which are parts of the great active principle. Beyond you am I, the adhyâtmâ, and that I which makes me one through all the motion of consciousness in time is always with Shiva. Do not then think of your consciousness as your real life ; do not imagine that it is something which enables you to live, for as a matter of fact even the higher consciousness is only a limitation ; it is only a body with which to explore time, and the I is beyond it. That is why some of the ancient philosophers said that I and God were one and the same, and yet they said " Neti, neti," that is " Not thus, not thus," whenever anyone proposed to describe that God or I in terms of matter or even in terms of consciousness. Even the person who has not distinguished between his body and his consciousness is conscious ; so also he who does not know that he knows that I still *is* I, even in the midst of the consciousness which he wrongly thinks to be the self. That is the I which is the same through all the three periods of time which are seen in the changing consciousness. To be that I without the consciousness is for him who is not yet a Mahâtmâ real sleep, that deep sleep out of which one comes rejoicing, experiencing unaccountable happiness. But that which to others is sleeping is waking to the Mahâtmâ.

Some slight glimpse of that I may be caught by all thoughtful persons if they will meditate on the following lines. When they look at their own bodies and those of others they can speak of each of them as " it ". When they look at the consciousness in another person they call that " you," but when they look at the consciousness in themselves they call it " I ". Why call the same thing by two different names ? Now, some make the mistake of thinking that they should say " I " to describe the, consciousness in another person. That is the illusion of the higher self. They must learn to say " you " when looking at the consciousness in themselves. Then the " I " will remain untainted by contact with the dual world, the man will be a Mahâtmâ. It was in this way that Shri Sankarâchârya used the " you " of Gautama Buddha.

One who has had a vision of this truth, or has realised it, looking back upon his human career will see that the personality and the body were a part of the material world. You were a part of the conscious world, a portion of something that was not your real self, but was the great consciousness to which no limits can be assigned. It was here that was to be found the reaping of all the sowing that was done within the limits of personality. Each new achievement brought an enlargement of consciousness, so that it became a bigger part of the universal consciousness than it was before.

In this you were a part of Vishnu, as in the personality a part of Brahmâ. Yet even this was not the end, however great became the expansion of your consciousness.

On all the seven rays consciousness may at last extend, as a result of experiences attained within the world of Brahmâ, so far as the immanence of Vishnu extends in that world, owing to the kind offices of mâyâ. But on the second ray it is possible to expand further still and be part of the transcendent aspect of Vishnu. Yet further may one go on the first ray in Vishnu's will, where he in turn is one with Shiva Himself. Here is the threshold of the true Nirvâna, when man rises above consciousness, as long before he rose above matter, and in that moment you will be no longer " you," but " I," and the universe grows " I ".

> If any teach NIRVANA is to cease,
>   Say unto such they lie.
> If any teach NIRVANA is to live,
>   Say unto such they err; not knowing this,
> Nor what light shines beyond their broken lamps.
>   Nor lifeless, timeless bliss.

GLOSSARY OF PRINCIPAL SANSKRIT WORDS
USED IN THIS BOOK

Ânanda : Happiness ; the state of real life.

Ananta : Endless time, the basis of consciousness.

Âtmâ : The ichchha in man.

Bhagavad-Gîtâ : The Song of the Lord, a devotional and philosophical treatise widely used by the Hindus.

Bhakti Yoga : Union with the divine by devotion to God.

Brahmâ : The third member of the divine trinity ; the world of things.

Brahman : God ; including real life, consciousness and things.

Buddhi : The jnana in man.

Chit : Consciousness.

Deva : A divine being of any grade ; one who shines from within. Vishnu is the supreme deva, the matrix of them all.

Dharma : The position of a soul on the ladder of evolution ; the law of its unfoldment.

Ichchhâ : The will in consciousness. Its active form is will ; its receptive form consciousness of self.

Jnâna : The wisdom of consciousness. Its active form is love ; its receptive form the consciousness of consciousness.

Karma :	Work ; action with intention. Also the law of reaction.
Kriyâ :	The activity of consciousness. Its active form is thought ; its receptive form consciousness of things.
Kriyâshakti :	Thought-power.
Lakshmî :	The goddess of prosperity ; wife of Vishnu. Especially connected with the sixth ray.
Manas :	The kriya in man.
Mâyâ :	Our life, a substitute for real life ; the world of relations between chit and sat.
Rajas :	The energy constituent of the world of things.
Sannyâsî :	One who is deliberately giving up mâyâ.
Sat :	Being ; the character of Brahmâ's world.
Sattva :	The law and order in the world of things ; the world of fixed ideas or material archetypes.
Shiva :	The first member of the trinity ; real life.
Shrî Krishna :	The great spiritual teacher of *The Bhagavad-Gîtâ ;* an incarnation of Vishnu.
Swayambhû :	The self-existent ; a name of God.
Tamas :	The matter constituent of the world of things.
Vijnâna :	Knowledge.
Vishnu :	The second member of the trinity. The world of consciousness.
Yoga :	Union with divine ; the means to that union.

Printed by A. K. Sitarama Shastri, at the Vasanta Press, Adyar, Madras.

CPSIA information can be obtained
at www.ICGtesting.com
Printed in the USA
LVHW092212081120
671112LV00037B/395